English
Olympiad

Class 08

A must have book for all
Olympiads & Talent Search Exams...

by
Amit Tanwar

BLOOM CAP
Bloom Cap Edu Ventures Pvt. Ltd.

Bloom Cap Edu Ventures Pvt. Ltd.

卐 **Administrative & Production Office**

'Ramchhaya' 4577/15, Agarwal Road, Darya Ganj, New Delhi -110002
Tele: 011- 47630600, 43518550

卐 **ISBN :** 978-93-25519-27-5

卐 **PRICE :** ₹100.00

卐 **PO No :** TXT-XX-XXXXXXX-X-XX

For further information about the books log on to
www.bloomcap.org

Follow us on   

Preface

"Future belongs to those Who prepares for it today"

School Olympiads are National & International level competitions conducted by different Government, Non-Government & Educational Organisations with the purpose of making the children ready to face competitive exams.

The challenging Questions asked in Olympiads motivate them to learn more & more and bring out the best results with improved academic performance. The Awards & Scholarship offered by Olympiads motivate children to aspire & strive for doing better and emerge out to be the best.

English Olympiads

English is one of the most widely spoken languages across the world. In today's era, good command over English is considered as a must have skill. The greatest advantage of studying English is improvement in communication skills along with the growth of personality.

English Olympiads are meant to strengthen students' command over this universal language by improving spellings, grammar, sentence structure and to master student's language skills.

'Bloom English Olympiad Study Book Class 8' is a perfect resource to Study & Practice for Olympiad Exams and other National & State Level Talent Search Exams & Other Competitions.

Some Special Features of Bloom English Olympiad Study Books are;

- Complete coverage of all the aspects of English; Grammar, Reading Comprehension, Writing Skills, Spellings, Vocabulary & Communication Skills.
- Chapterwise Exercises having different types of Objective Questions at par with the Olympiad Level.
- Olympiad Pattern Practice Sets at the end.

This book is prepared by Expert Panel with the utmost care, still if you have any suggestions regarding its improvement then feel free to contact us at olympiads@bloomcap.org. We will try to inculcate your suggestions in the further editions.

Contents

Nouns

1 Mark Questions

Directions (Q. Nos. 1-6) Read the sentences given below and choose the option that contain nouns.

1. They're digging a new swimming pool in the park.
   (a) Digging, new, park
   (b) Swimming pool, park
   (c) Digging, park
   (d) New, swimming pool

2. The Chinese army adopted cleverness to win the war and occupy India's territory.
   (a) Chinese, army, cleverness
   (b) Army, cleverness, war, territory
   (c) War, India, territory, adopted
   (d) Cleverness, army, war

3. The Government of India is in favour of poor and marginalised sections of society.
   (a) Government, India, favour
   (b) Society, sections, poor
   (c) Poor, society, favour
   (d) Society, poor, India

4. We have received no information about the accident that took place near the hospital.
   (a) Received, information, accident
   (b) Hospital, accident, near
   (c) Information, place, near
   (d) Information, accident, hospital

5. I heard this news in the morning about the President of America.
   (a) Heard, news, morning
   (b) About, President, America
   (c) News, President, America
   (d) Morning, heard, about

6. Doctor said that we can prevent a heart-attack by eating properly and getting enough exercise.
   (a) Prevent, eating, properly
   (b) Doctor, heart-attack, exercise
   (c) Eating, enough, exercise
   (d) Doctor, eating, prevent, properly

Directions (Q. Nos. 7-13) Choose the correct form of noun from the options.

7. A large .... is expected.
   (a) crowd   (b) crowds
   (c) crowded   (d) creed

8. The pair of .... is good.
   (a) shoe
   (b) shoes
   (c) Both (a) and (b)
   (d) None of the above

9. These .... were found there.
   (a) gloves   (b) glove
   (c) pair of gloves (d) None of these

10. The .... need sharpening.
    (a) scissors   (b) scissor
    (c) pair of scissors (d) None of these

11. We should give .... to the poor.
  (a) almost
  (b) alms
  (c) everything
  (d) kindness

12. Please buy two .... from the store.
  (a) juice cans
  (b) juices
  (c) bunch of juices
  (d) None of these

13. He was giving her .... when the phone rang.
  (a) advice
  (b) advices
  (c) advised
  (d) None of these

Directions (Q. Nos. 14-20) Which type of noun are the underlined words? Choose from the options given below.

14. I am travelling to <u>Dubai</u> for the first time.
  (a) Collective Noun
  (b) Abstract Noun
  (c) Concrete Noun
  (d) Proper Noun

15. <u>Water</u> is a driving force of all nature.
  (a) Collective Noun
  (b) Abstract Noun
  (c) Concrete Noun
  (d) Proper Noun

16. The <u>bouquet</u> of flowers is wilting, even though it was labelled as fresh.
  (a) Collective Noun
  (b) Abstract Noun
  (c) Concrete Noun
  (d) Proper Noun

17. I'd like the <u>freedom</u> to travel all over the world.
  (a) Collective Noun
  (b) Abstract Noun
  (c) Concrete Noun
  (d) Proper Noun

18. The responsibility of <u>tolerance</u> lies with those who have the wider vision.
  (a) Collective Noun
  (b) Abstract Noun
  (c) Concrete Noun
  (d) Proper Noun

19. The <u>picture</u> you painted is very pretty.
  (a) Collective Noun
  (b) Abstract Noun
  (c) Concrete Noun
  (d) Proper Noun

20. He had a thick <u>bundle</u> of envelopes under his arm.
  (a) Collective Noun
  (b) Abstract Noun
  (c) Concrete Noun
  (d) Proper Noun

21. Cases of Srinagar and Chennai shows that there has been little attempt to deal with floods beyond providing a relief.
  Which among the following noun is mentioned in the above lines?
  (a) Common Noun
  (b) Proper Noun
  (c) Concrete Noun
  (d) Both (a) and (b)

Directions (Q. Nos. 22-24) Replace the underlined words with the correct nouns in the given sentences. Choose from the options.

22. A <u>litter</u> of sheep were straying all over the road causing confusion in the <u>cars</u>.
  (a) Flock, cycles
  (b) Flock, traffic
  (c) Pack, cycles
  (d) Pack, traffic

23. Rohan prefers to do his <u>discovery</u> on the radio.
  (a) Wisdom, software
  (b) Wisdom, internet
  (c) Research, internet
  (d) Research, software

24. That <u>girls</u> grew up to be the greatest painter in <u>city</u>.
  (a) Boys, country
  (b) Boy, Florence
  (c) Men, Florence
  (d) Man, country

25. Choose the correct abstract form of noun 'sane' from the given options.
  (a) Sinful
  (b) Sin
  (c) Sanity
  (d) Sensible

2 Marks Questions

26. Match the following.

List-I (Collective Noun)	List-II (Common Noun)
A. A regiment of	1. Bees
B. A cloud of	2. Pearls
C. A swarm of	3. Soldiers
D. A string of	4. Insects

Codes

	A	B	C	D		A	B	C	D
(a)	1	2	3	4	(b)	4	3	2	1
(c)	3	4	1	2	(d)	2	3	4	1

27. Match the following nouns to make a correct compound noun.

List-I	List-II
A. Brain	1. Pipe
B. Count	2. Storm
C. Drain	3. Way
D. Drive	4. Down

Codes

	A	B	C	D		A	B	C	D
(a)	1	2	3	4	(b)	2	3	4	1
(c)	2	4	1	3	(d)	4	3	2	1

Directions (Q. Nos. 28 and 29) Read the passage given below and fill in the blanks with nouns.

Books are very useful to us. They are the best ....**28(i)**.... of man. They never cheat the reader. Books are a good source of knowledge. We get ....**28(ii)**.... on different subjects. We can read books of our taste. They enlighten our ....**29(i)**.... and make us bold to face the realities and difficulties of ....**29(ii)**.... . We can find everything in books.

28. (i) (a) Companion (b) Family
　　　(c) Neighbour (d) Neighbours

28. (ii) (a) Know (b) Inform
　　　(c) Knowledge (d) Informations

29. (i) (a) Bodies (b) Hearts
　　　(c) Body (d) Head

29. (ii) (a) Life (b) Lives
　　　(c) Death (d) Deaths

30. Match the following.

List-I (Masculine Noun)	List-II (Feminine Noun)
A. Wizard	1. Goose
B. Nephew	2. Witch
C. Gander	3. Vixen
D. Fox	4. Niece

Codes

	A	B	C	D		A	B	C	D
(a)	1	3	2	4	(b)	2	4	3	1
(c)	4	2	3	1	(d)	2	4	1	3

31. Match the following.

List-I (Types of Noun)		List-II (Examples)
A. Uncountable Noun	1.	We have to get at the truth of the matter.
B. Abstract Noun	2.	He broke the plate I gave him to put of the table.
C. Common Noun	3.	Consumption of alcohol is injurious to health.
D. Compound Noun	4.	Rainwater harvesting helps to increase the underground water level.

Codes

	A	B	C	D		A	B	C	D
(a)	1	3	4	2	(b)	3	1	2	4
(c)	4	2	3	1	(d)	2	4	1	3

Chapter 02

Pronouns

1 Mark Questions

Directions (Q. Nos. 1-7) Identify the type of (underlined pronoun) used in the following sentences.

1. <u>Many</u> of them came, but few stayed long.
   (a) Reflexive Pronoun
   (b) Personal Pronoun
   (c) Indefinite Pronoun
   (d) Reciprocal Pronoun

2. They helped <u>one another</u> in solving the puzzle.
   (a) Reflexive Pronoun
   (b) Personal Pronoun
   (c) Reciprocal Pronoun
   (d) Indefinite Pronoun

3. <u>All</u> of <u>those</u> are expensive.
   (a) Indefinite and Demonstrative Pronoun
   (b) Possessive and Reflexive Pronoun
   (c) Reciprocal and Personal Pronoun
   (d) Indefinite and Personal Pronoun

4. Did <u>they</u> teach <u>themselves</u> how to speak French?
   (a) Personal and Demonstrative Pronoun
   (b) Indefinite and Reciprocal Pronoun
   (c) Personal and Reflexive Pronoun
   (d) Possessive and Interrogative Pronoun

5. <u>I</u> know the girl <u>whose</u> name is Jia.
   (a) Reflexive and Personal Pronoun
   (b) Personal and Relative Pronoun
   (c) Indefinite and Reciprocal Pronoun
   (d) Demonstrative and Interrogative Pronoun

6. <u>What</u> did you bring for <u>me</u> in lunch?
   (a) Interrogative and Personal Pronoun
   (b) Reflexive and Personal Pronoun
   (c) Relative and Reflexive Pronoun
   (d) Reciprocal and Indefinite Pronoun

7. This is the man <u>whose</u> horse <u>you</u> stole.
   (a) Reflexive and Relative Pronoun
   (b) Indefinite and Reflexive Pronoun
   (c) Relative and Personal Pronoun
   (d) Reciprocal and Demonstrative Pronoun

Directions (Q. Nos. 8-16) Fill in the blanks with suitable pronouns.

8. People .... eat too much die early.
   (a) that   (b) who   (c) whom   (d) which

9. This is the place .... Vasco da Gama landed.
   (a) that   (b) which   (c) where   (d) who

10. That was the reason .... I failed the test.
    (a) that   (b) which   (c) where   (d) why

11. .... who purchased one of the paintings was pleased.
    - (a) Someone   (b) Everyone
    - (c) Anybody   (d) Somebody

12. We are going to have a party. We're going to invite all .... friends.
    - (a) our   (b) their
    - (c) its   (d) your

13. Do you think most people are happy in .... jobs?
    - (a) our   (b) their
    - (c) your   (d) it

14. I know Mr. Watson, but I don't know .... wife.
    - (a) his   (b) her   (c) their   (d) its

15. I'm going to wash .... hair before I go out.
    - (a) mine   (b) me
    - (c) my   (d) myself

16. The students were so noisy. Even Nancy and Neha were making a lot of noise ....
    - (a) herself   (b) itself
    - (c) themselves   (d) myself

Directions (Q. Nos. 17-21) Replace the nouns in the given sentences with pronouns.

17. You and your friends are going to get into trouble if you and your friends persist in calling your neighbour names.
    - (a) You are going to get into trouble if you persist in calling them names.
    - (b) You all are going to get trouble if they persist in calling our neighbour names.
    - (c) They are going to get them troubled if you persist on calling him names.
    - (d) Those are going to get in trouble if he persists on calling their names.

18. Mia and Jane performed in the talent show.
    - (a) They performed in the talent show.
    - (b) Those performed in the talent show.
    - (c) Them performed in the talent show.
    - (d) None of the above

19. My father told my brother not to make this mistake again.
    - (a) He told my brother not to make this mistake again.
    - (b) He told them not to make it again.
    - (c) He told him not to make it again.
    - (d) Father told them not to make this again.

20. My sister and I decided to visit my aunt this weekend.
    - (a) Me and my sister decided to visit my aunt this weekend.
    - (b) They decided to visit her aunt this weekend.
    - (c) We decided to visit aunt this weekend.
    - (d) We decided to visit her this weekend.

21. Don't tell Lily and Sally that Paul and I have forgotten to bring the list.
    - (a) Don't tell them what I and my friends have forgotten to bring it.
    - (b) Don't tell them that we have forgotten to bring it.
    - (c) Don't tell there that they have forgotten to bring that.
    - (d) Don't tell these that they have forgotten to bring them.

2 Marks Questions

22. Read the short passage given below and fill in the blanks with pronouns.

Sarojini Naidu was educated in .... early years under her father's own care. .... wanted her to become a great mathematician or scientist but she loved to dream and write poems. .... was hardly eleven when she wrote her first poem.

(a) her, He, She   (b) hers, She, He
(c) hers, He, She   (d) her, She, He

23. Match the following.

List-I (Types of Pronoun)	List-II (Examples)
A. Indefinite Pronoun	1. I lost my pen in the library. Can I have one of <u>yours</u>?
B. Demonstrative Pronoun	2. Here are the keys <u>that</u> you were searching for.
C. Relative Pronoun	3. <u>These</u> are nice shoes, but they look uncomfortable.
D. Possessive Pronoun	4. Would you like to go <u>somewhere</u> this weekend?

Codes

	A	B	C	D		A	B	C	D
(a)	1	2	3	4	(b)	2	4	1	3
(c)	4	3	2	1	(d)	3	1	4	2

24. Choose the option that correctly replaces the nouns in the given sentence with pronouns.

Mrs. Mehra is my father's boss and because of my father's hardwork, Mrs. Mehra respects my father a lot.

(a) Mrs. Mehra is my father's boss and because of their hardwork, they respect him a lot.

(b) Mrs. Mehra is my father's boss and because of their hardwork, she respects them a lot.

(c) She is my his boss and because of his hardwork, she respects them a lot.

(d) She is his boss and because of his hardwork, she respects him a lot.

25. Match the following.

List-I (Nouns)	List-II (Pronouns)
A. Rahul and Sunny's	1. We
B. My friends and I	2. Theirs
C. Chris	3. Itself
D. Dog	4. He

Codes

	A	B	C	D		A	B	C	D
(a)	1	3	2	4	(b)	2	1	4	3
(c)	2	1	3	4	(d)	4	2	3	1

Directions (Q. Nos. 26 and 27) Read the passage given below and replace the underlined words with appropriate pronouns.

Trees are incredibly significant in <u>your</u> **26(i)** life. Life will turn out to be extremely troublesome without trees. We can say <u>these</u> **26(ii)** life would be done because a tree is the most significant thing giving us a solid and healthy life. <u>Those</u> **27(i)** days individual are eagerly chopping down trees; on the off chance that this continues, one day will come when <u>she</u> **27(ii)** will have no trees left with us.

26. (i) (a) their   (b) her
     (c) our   (d) his

26. (ii) (a) that   (b) this
     (c) those   (d) them

27. (i) (a) this   (b) those
     (c) these   (d) they

27. (ii) (a) he   (b) we
     (c) us   (d) them

Chapter 03

Verbs

1 Mark Questions

Directions (Q. Nos. 1-5) Read the sentences and identify the type of verb of underlined word.

1. He <u>became</u> a successful lawyer.
   (a) Transitive Verb (b) Intransitive Verb
   (c) Linking Verb (d) Modal Verb

2. I <u>could</u> recognise him with great difficulty.
   (a) Transitive Verb (b) Intransitive Verb
   (c) Linking Verb (d) Modal Verb

3. My father <u>took</u> me to the movies for my birthday.
   (a) Transitive Verb (b) Intransitive Verb
   (c) Linking Verb (d) Modal Verb

4. Susan <u>lives</u> on the east side of the city.
   (a) Linking Verb (b) Transitive Verb
   (c) Intransitive Verb (d) Modal Verb

5. Children <u>must</u> do their homework.
   (a) Linking Verb
   (b) Transitive Verb
   (c) Intransitive Verb
   (d) Modal Verb

Directions (Q. Nos. 6-12) Fill in the blanks with the correct modal verbs from the given options.

6. Rohan went to Agra last week. He .... come today.
   (a) may (b) might
   (c) would (d) can

7. Had he worked hard, he .... have passed the examination.
   (a) might (b) could
   (c) would (d) shall

8. I .... be thankful to you if you help me at this time of need.
   (a) can (b) shall
   (c) would (d) could

9. His mentor helped him in his research work so that he .... complete it in time.
   (a) should (b) would
   (c) could (d) might

10. She endeavoured her best to surpass the target but she .... not.
    (a) may (b) could
    (c) can (d) might

11. I assure you that I shall help you in this matter if I ....
    (a) can (b) could
    (c) may (d) might

12. Children .... respect their elders and get their blessings.
    (a) can (b) could
    (c) must (d) would

Directions (Q. Nos. 13-18) In each of the following sentences, the underlined verb may be inappropriately used. Choose the correct option from the given options.

13. The entire audience <u>bursting</u> out in a hilarious laughter as she said the punch line.

    (a) Burst
    (b) Could burst
    (c) Can burst
    (d) Would burst

14. I think, she has deliberately <u>switched</u> the mobile off.

    (a) Switch
    (b) Would switch
    (c) Can switch
    (d) No correction required

15. Their flight may <u>taking</u> off after half an hour if the weather permits.

    (a) Taken   (b) Take
    (c) May take   (d) Can take

16. How does a butterfly <u>gets</u> its colour?

    (a) Get   (b) Will get
    (c) Got   (d) Can got

17. I have <u>scrutinising</u> the area thoroughly. There is no mischievous thing there.

    (a) Will scrutinise   (b) Scrutinised
    (c) Can scrutinise   (d) Would Scrutinise

18. She <u>thinking</u> it would rather sound silly than defensive.

    (a) Think   (b) Will think
    (c) Thought   (d) Can Think

2 Marks Questions

19. Read the passage and change the form of verb underlined below.

    The man called Boone woke up at the crack of dawn and <u>to make</u> his way to the pier. His assistant was already packing the fishing net as the boat gently bobbed in the calm waters.

    "What <u>to do</u> it look like Jon?" asked Boone.

    "The forecast mentions a quiet start to the day with a spell of rain to come later on in the afternoon."

    (i) In the given passage, <u>to make</u> will be changed to ....
        (a) Make
        (b) Makes
        (c) Made
        (d) Can make

    (ii) "What <u>to do</u> it look like Jon?" will be changed to ....
        (a) What does it look like Jon?
        (b) What can do it look like Jon?
        (c) What could do it look like Jon?
        (d) What will do it look like Jon?

20. Read the passage given below and choose the option with the verbs.

    Tennis is a game played with a felt-shrouded elastic ball, a tennis racket, and a court. Since 1998, each 23rd September has been designated "Tennis Day". Tennis' proper name is "grass tennis". In the first place, from the get-go in the eleventh century, major parts in France played a game like this with their hands. It was classified as "Jeu de Paume". In the fifteenth century, the players played with rackets. Presently, it is classified as "tennis".

    (a) is, classified, get-go
    (b) played, is, classified, been, century
    (c) is, played, has been designated, was
    (d) get-go, is, was, century

21. Fill in the blanks with appropriate forms of verbs from the options given below.

Technology .... our life simpler, but it has also .... a dramatic increase in pollution. This pollution of air, water, soil, noise and light .... to myriad of problems.

(a) have made, cause, had led
(b) has make, cause, have lead
(c) had make, caused, had lead
(d) has made, caused, has led

22. Replace the underlined words with appropriate verbs from the options given below.

Food <u>are</u> the necessity of life. It <u>will provide</u> nutrition, sustenance and growth to human body. Food <u>must</u> be classified into cereals, pulses, nuts and oilseeds, vegetables, fruits, milk and milk products and fresh food. Most of the food items <u>contained</u> protein, fat, carbohydrates, vitamins and water in varying amounts.

(a) is, provided, will, contain
(b) is, provide, will, contains
(c) is, provides, can, contains
(d) is, provides, can, contain

23. Consider the following statements.

1. She was travelling around the world this time next week.
2. He has been working in this garage for eight years.

Which of these statements is/are grammatically correct?

(a) Only 1
(b) Only 2
(c) Both 1 and 2
(d) None of the above

24. Read the passage given below and replace the underlined words with correct modal verbs.

Plants need sunlight and water to make their food. You <u>must</u> do an experiment to test if this is true. Place a bucket over a patch of green grass. After a few days, lift the bucket. You <u>could</u> see that the grass is not as green anymore. If you leave the bucket in place for a week, the grass will become very dull. This happens because the grass cannot make food in the dark. Remove the bucket. In a few days, the grass will start turning green again.

(i) In the given passage, <u>must</u> will be changed to ....

(a) can   (b) need
(c) would   (d) will

(ii) In the given passage, <u>could</u> will be changed to ....

(a) must
(b) might
(c) will
(d) may

Chapter 04

Adverbs

1 Mark Questions

Directions (Q. Nos. 1-6) Identify the type of adverb given in the following sentence.

1. Aren't you hungry? You've hardly touched your dinner.
   (a) Relative Adverb
   (b) Adverb of Place
   (c) Adverb of Degree
   (d) Adverb of Reason

2. I haven't been going to the gym lately.
   (a) Adverb of Time
   (b) Adverb of Degree
   (c) Adverb of Place
   (d) Adverb of Reason

3. We went into the cave, and there were bats everywhere!
   (a) Adverb of Degree
   (b) Relative Adverb
   (c) Adverb of Place
   (d) Sentence Adverb

4. I politely opened the door for my grandmother as she stepped out of the car.
   (a) Adverb of Degree
   (b) Adverb of Manner
   (c) Adverb of Place
   (d) Adverb of Time

5. I rarely eat fast food these days.
   (a) Adverb of Frequency
   (b) Adverb of Degree
   (c) Relative Adverb
   (d) Sentence Adverb

6. Nobody knows the reason why Amit behaved that way.
   (a) Adverb of Degree
   (b) Adverb of Place
   (c) Relative Adverb
   (d) Sentence Adverb

Directions (Q. Nos. 7-12) Fill in the blanks by choosing the appropriate adverbs.

7. The driver of the car was .... injured.
   (a) frequently   (b) seriously
   (c) willingly   (d) carefully

8. The young soldier folded his clothes .... in a pile at the end of his bunk.
   (a) neatly   (b) hence
   (c) regularly   (d) early

9. He .... accepted the invitation from his neighbour.
   (a) frequently   (b) graciously
   (c) slowly   (d) already

10. The class .... went for the fieldtrips.

    (a) totally   (b) extremely

    (c) rarely   (d) ideally

11. The audience were .... spell bound. They liked the speech .... much.

    (a) very, extremely

    (b) a little, highly

    (c) extremely, very

    (d) a little, often

12. She sings .... well. She can try her hand at singing.

    (a) pretty   (b) a bit

    (c) a little   (d) None of these

Directions (Q. Nos. 13-18) Improve the sentences given below by changing its underlined portion.

13. Do you <u>somewhere</u> visit your grandma?

    (a) Sometimes   (b) A little

    (c) Graciously   (d) Highly

14. That picture was taken in the park <u>hence</u> I used to play.

    (a) Why   (b) So

    (c) When   (d) Where

15. The teachers and mentors are working <u>how much</u> on the project.

    (a) Hard   (b) Sometimes

    (c) Occasionally   (d) Very

16. Pack some food stuff for the journey, <u>slightly</u> you get hungry.

    (a) Accidently   (b) Very

    (c) Extremely   (d) Lest

17. The happiness we seek lies <u>inside</u> of our materialistic obsessions.

    (a) Downwards   (b) Outside

    (c) Near   (d) Towards

18. The wind was moving <u>outside</u>, making it difficult for climbers.

    (a) Downwards   (b) Near

    (c) Towards   (d) Inside

2 Marks Questions

Directions (Q. Nos. 19 and 20) Read the passage and fill in the blanks with an appropriate adverb.

I had a ......**19(i)**........ dream last night. I was in a garden. It was getting dark and it was ......**19(ii)**........ cold. My head was aching badly. I was walking out of the garden when suddenly I saw a girl sitting on a seat. She seemed very unhappy. She looked up and smiled ......**20(i)**........ at me. I felt anxious for some reason. I wanted to be friendly so I tried hard to think of something to say. But I couldn't. I just stood there ......**20(ii)**........ .

19. (i) (a) strangely   (b) strange

       (c) sudden   (d) suddenly

19. (ii) (a) terribly   (b) terrible

       (c) outside   (d) persistent

20. (i) (a) polite   (b) sadly

      (c) a little   (d) a bit

20. (ii) (a) extremely

      (b) foolish

      (c) foolishly

      (d) sufficiently

21. Consider the following statements.

    1. Sandra fluently waited to hear the news as to whether or not she was accepted into the science program.

    2. The clerk very politely explained that the item I wanted to return would not be accepted without a receipt.

Which of these statements is/are grammatically correct?

(a) Only 1
(b) Only 2
(c) Both 1 and 2
(d) None of these

22. Read the passage given below and choose the option with the adverbs.

Shruti listened carefully to the messenger's tale, and then she laid aside her broom and slowly gazed at her rough, ruined hands. "Oh yes, I can tell you what this means," she said, and she gradually smiled for the first time in three long years.

(a) Carefully, slowly, rough, ruined
(b) Slowly, gazed, first, three
(c) Carefully, aside, rough, gazed
(d) Carefully, aside, slowly, gradually

23. Replace the underlined words with suitable adverbs.

It was Christmas Eve and children everywhere were <u>slowly</u> awaiting Santa's arrival. The elves worked <u>hardly</u> to put the finishing touches on all the toys. The shiny reindeer <u>lately</u> ran into position at the head of Santa's sleigh.

(a) Hungry, glad, rapidly
(b) Today, eagerly, quick
(c) Hungrily, eagerly, quickly
(d) Today, gladly, rapid

24. Match the following.

List-I (Types of Adverb)	Lise-II (Example)
A. Adverb of Time	1. You have to push the peddle down to speed up.
B. Relative Adverb	2. The child ran towards his mother happily.
C. Adverb of Place	3. They will rehearse for the show tonight.
D. Adverb of Manner	4. Can you tell me the time when the manager may come?

Codes

	A	B	C	D		A	B	C	D
(a)	1	2	3	4	(b)	3	4	1	2
(c)	2	1	3	4	(d)	4	3	2	1

25. Consider the following statements.

1. She held her hat tightly in the strong wind.
2. You look tired. Didn't you sleep good?
3. Alex danced loudly around the playground.

Which of these statements is/are grammatically correct?

(a) 1 and 2
(b) 1 and 3
(c) 2 and 3
(d) Only 1

Adjectives

1 Mark Questions

Directions (Q. Nos. 1-6) Replace the underlined words with suitable adjectives.

1. My dad was <u>scare</u> when he picked up the skunk.
   (a) Bravery   (b) Courageous
   (c) Valour   (d) Courage

2. Many of earth's <u>greater</u> wonders have been labeled as <u>history</u> monuments.
   (a) great, historic
   (b) greatest, historical
   (c) greater, historical
   (d) greatest, historic

3. The <u>taller</u> man at the counter felt that John was a very <u>gentle</u> gentleman.
   (a) more tall, bad
   (b) taller, kinder
   (c) tallest, worst
   (d) tallest, kind

4. The dog is <u>energetic</u> than the elephant.
   (a) most energetic
   (b) more energy
   (c) more energetic
   (d) energetic

5. The department order says that no one will leave the station till <u>far</u> notice.
   (a) more far   (b) further
   (c) furthest   (d) more further

6. <u>Blue</u> and <u>Black</u> colour pens should be avoided while making notes.
   (a) Black, White   (b) Green, Blue
   (c) Red, Green   (d) Red, Violet

Directions (Q. Nos. 7-12) Fill in the blanks with suitable adjectives.

7. I think Pakistan will win the match but only .... people agree with me.
   (a) few   (b) little
   (c) many   (d) a lot of

8. How .... fruit do you eat in an average day?
   (a) many   (b) much
   (c) some   (d) any

9. She dedicates .... time to her homework than to her hobbies.
   (a) little   (b) a little
   (c) less   (d) any

10. I have .... interest in classical music.
    (a) little   (b) few
    (c) less   (d) any

11. In the last holidays I read a good book, but father gave me an even ....one last weekend.
    (a) best   (b) better
    (c) most better   (d) more better

12. She always arrives .... than her teacher.

   (a) late   (b) more late

   (c) most late   (d) later

13. Choose the simile to complete the sentence from the given options.

   Her smile is .... the Sun.

   (a) hot like   (b) as bright as

   (c) as pretty as   (d) as wide as

14. Fill in the blank with the correct order of adjectives from the options.

   I was thrilled to receive a .... book with my order.

   (a) Big, beautiful, leather-bound

   (b) Leather-bound, big, beautiful

   (c) Beautiful big leather-bound

   (d) None of the above

15. Choose the comparative adjective in the following sentence.

   (a) This is probably the longest one I've ever seen.

   (b) This list is longer than the last one.

   (c) Stop acting so weird with your siblings.

   (d) Have some chocolate cake with your friends.

16. Choose the superlative adjective in the given sentence.

   (a) This is the fastest car I've ever driven.

   (b) The grass is greener on the other side.

   (c) Our house is bigger than our grandmother's is.

   (d) The box was blue, and oddly shaped.

17. Which sentence uses the correct order of adjectives?

   (a) We took a ride on a red, new, Italian motorbike.

   (b) We took a ride on an Italian, new, red motorbike.

   (c) We took a ride on a new, red, Italian motorbike.

   (d) None of the above

18. Which sentence uses the correct order of adjectives?

   (a) I've been shopping for the Japanese long sushi chopsticks.

   (b) I've been shopping for the long Japanese sushi chopsticks.

   (c) I've been shipping for the long sushi Japanese chopsticks.

   (d) None of the above

2 Marks Questions

19. Consider the following statements.

   1. The nearer school is five kilometres from this village.

   2. Her condition is now worse than what it was before.

   In which of the above statements, adjective is used correctly?

   (a) Only 1

   (b) Only 2

   (c) Both 1 and 2

   (d) None of the above

20. Match the following.

List-I (Positive Degree of Adjectives)	List-II (Superlative Degree of Adjectives)
A. Proper	1. Worst
B. Good	2. Latest
C. Late	3. Best
D. Bad	4. Most Proper

Codes

	A	B	C	D		A	B	C	D
(a)	1	2	3	4	(b)	2	3	4	1
(c)	4	3	2	1	(d)	3	1	4	2

21. Read the passage given below and choose the option with the adjectives.

My most valuable possession stands proudly in the corner of my small, purple bedroom. The old guitar sounds like rain drops drumming the window and the copper strings streches all the way down.

(a) valuable, small, strings

(b) valuable, small, purple, old, copper

(c) proudly, valuable, old, copper

(d) proudly, small, purple, strings

22. Replace the underlined words with appropriate adjectives.

"These is the ground where Amit said the match will be held," said Rohit. "Good, we found it!" said Aarav, "Which time did he say the match would begin?" "At 5:30," replied Rohit, "Let's go inside. Amit is probably already inside with all his envious teammates."

(a) This, What, amazing

(b) That, When, worthless

(c) This, When, amazing

(d) That, What, worthless

23. Fill in the blanks with appropriate adjectives from the options given below.

The beautifully .... sweater was made by hand. Thus, it costed more than the .... kind of sweater.

(a) Embroidery, store-buy

(b) Embroider, store-bought

(c) Embroidered, store-buy

(d) Embroidered, store-bought

24. Match the following to fill in the blanks with appropriate adjectives.

List-I	List-II
A. These	1. I cannot give you money at ...... moment.
B. That	2. In .... matters, the only certainty is that nothing is certain.
C. This	3. .... people were mean to her.
D. Those	4. Will you please grant me .... loan we talked about?

Codes

	A	B	C	D		A	B	C	D
(a)	2	4	1	3	(b)	4	2	1	3
(c)	2	4	3	1	(d)	4	2	3	1

25. Consider the following statements.

1. Father seemed filled with the .... anger against him.

2. We were about to be thrown into the .... and bitterest battle of the war.

3. The night when the storm was at its .... , the girl begged her father to stay with her.

Which of the following options can be used to fill in the blanks in all of these statements?

(a) Fierce   (b) More Fierce

(c) Fiercest   (d) Most fierce

26. Consider the following statements.

1. That geyser dominated the bathroom like a .... monster.

2. The .... winds seemed about to tear the ship to pieces.

3. The political entities of the twentieth century are the survivors of a .... rivalry.

Which of the following options can be used to fill in the blanks in all of these statements?

(a) Ferocious   (b) More ferocious

(c) Most ferocious   (d) Ferociousest

Articles

1 Mark Questions

Directions (Q. Nos. 1-10) Fill in the blanks with suitable articles.

1. He belongs to .... different school of thought.
   (a) a
   (b) an
   (c) the
   (d) No article

2. Do you know where .... library is?
   (a) a
   (b) an
   (c) the
   (d) No article

3. Yours is .... inspiring story which must be known to people.
   (a) a
   (b) an
   (c) the
   (d) No article

4. I lived on .... Main Street when I first came to this town.
   (a) a
   (b) an
   (c) the
   (d) No article

5. .... fumes of cars and factories are .... primary reasons for air pollution.
   (a) The, a
   (b) A, an
   (c) An, the
   (d) The, the

6. When mom was ill, ... lot of her friends came to .... hospital to visit her.
   (a) a, the
   (b) an, a
   (c) the, a
   (d) the, an

7. Mr. Gokhale is .... honorary President of our society.
   (a) a
   (b) an
   (c) the
   (d) No article

8. We listen to .... English CD although she has .... exercise book.
   (a) a, the
   (b) a, an
   (c) an, an
   (d) the, an

9. Lake Superior is .... largest of .... Great Lakes.
   (a) a, the
   (b) a, an
   (c) the, a
   (d) the, the

10. Our uncle lives in .... Philippines. It is .... beautiful place to visit.
    (a) the, a
    (b) a, an
    (c) an, a
    (d) a, the

Directions (Q. Nos. 11-16) Replace the underlined articles with the correct articles from the options given below.

11. <u>The</u> oval is shaped like <u>the</u> egg.
    (a) An, an
    (b) An, the
    (c) The, a
    (d) The, an

12. In <u>a</u> game of chess, a pawn can be promoted to <u>the</u> queen.
(a) The, a   (b) The, an
(c) An, an   (d) A, a

13. He spilled <u>a</u> milk all over <u>a</u> floor.
(a) the, a   (b) a, the
(c) The, the   (d) a, an

14. She asked me to complete <u>an</u> project by <u>an</u> evening.
(a) a, a   (b) the, a
(c) the, the   (d) an, a

15. The architect designed only <u>an</u> single door in <u>a</u> hall.
(a) the, an   (b) a, the
(c) the, a   (d) the, the

16. My father is <u>a</u> employee in <u>a</u> municipal office.
(a) an, a   (b) the, a
(c) an, the   (d) the, the

17. Improve the sentence given below by changing its underlined portion.
The answer to all the sufferings of human beings <u>lies in the science</u>.
(a) Lies in science   (b) Lies in a science
(c) Lies in an science (d) None of these

18. Improve the sentence given below by changing its underlined portion.
The earthquake derailed the lives of many people but <u>in an year time</u> leaving apart the victims, no one remembered anything.
(a) in the year time (b) in a year time
(c) in year time   (d) None of these

19. Improve the paragraph by changing its underlined portion.
Once upon a time there lived an ant. The ant was very young. The ant wanted to learn how to collect food. Therefore, the ant approached an ant who was skilled in collecting food. <u>A second ant agreed to teach a first ant a skill she wanted to learn.</u>
(a) The second ant agreed to teach the first ant the skill she wanted to learn.
(b) The second ant agreed to teach a first ant a skill she wanted to learn.
(c) A second ant agreed to teach an first ant an skill she wanted to learn.
(d) A second ant agreed to teach a first ant an skill she wanted to learn.

2 Marks Questions

20. Fill in the blanks to complete the passage given below.
There was a tiny squirrel. It was climbing .... high mountain. A foolish tortoise was following her. There was .... hard shell on his back. Suddenly a strong wind began to blow. .... squirrel ran fast. .... tortoise could not run fast so he was sad.
(a) the, a, the, a
(b) a, a, the, the
(c) the, the, a, a
(d) a, the, a, the

21. Match the following.

List-I	List-II
A. The	1. Umbrella
B. An	2. Sun
C. A	3. Cup of tea
D. An	4. Honest person

Codes

	A	B	C	D
(a)	1	2	3	4
(b)	2	1	3	4
(c)	4	3	1	2
(d)	3	2	1	4

22. Read the passage given below and choose the option with the articles.

Surat is a large city beside the Tapi River in the West Indian state of Gujarat. Surat was known to be a popular port in the ancient times and even now, it is famous.

(a) the, the, a, the   (b) a, the, the, a, the

(c) a, the, a, the   (d) a, the, the, a

23. Match the following to fill in the blanks with articles.

List I		List II
A.	A	1. Delhi Railway Junction is one of .... biggest stations in the country.
B.	An	2. Delhi has .... unique International Museum of Toilets.
C.	The	3. Delhi is .... old city and capital of India.
D.	No article	4. Delhi is divided into .... Old Delhi and New Delhi.

Codes

	A	B	C	D		A	B	C	D
(a)	3	2	4	1	(b)	2	3	1	4
(c)	1	4	3	2	(d)	4	2	3	1

24. Which of the following sentences has the correct usage of articles?

(a) She found herself in trouble when she saw no auto outside a station.

(b) Mr. Sharma became the Principal of the school in 2015.

(c) I would like to talk to one of a managers.

(d) Most of a people of Northern India do not know Telugu.

25. Consider the following statements.

1. We usually meet on the Monday.

2. People will travel to a Mars soon.

Which of these statements is/are incorrect?

(a) Only 1

(b) Only 2

(c) Both 1 and 2

(d) None of the above

26. Read the passage and replace the underlined articles with correct articles from the options given below.

The Great Barrier Reef is <u>an</u> world's biggest coral reef and has 2900 smaller reefs joined onto it. It covers over 850 islands and stretches over 2600 kilometres. It supports <u>an</u> wide diversity of life and was selected as <u>the</u> World Heritage Site in 1981. The Great Barrier Reef is so big that it can be seen from outer space and is <u>an</u> world's biggest structure made entirely of living organisms.

(a) the, a, a, the   (b) the, a, the, the

(c) a, a, the, the   (d) a, the, the, a

27. Consider the following statements.

1. Scuffles broke out between rival supporters during .... Ice Hockey tournament.

2. The stunt brought shocked gasps from .... audience.

Choose the option that can be used to fill in both the blanks.

(a) a   (b) the

(c) an   (d) No article

Chapter 07

Prepositions

1 Mark Questions

Directions (Q. Nos. 1-7) Fill in the blanks by choosing the correct prepositions of time from the given options.

1. Lata had promised to be back .... five o'clock.
(a) in   (b) by
(c) past   (d) ago

2. The dinosaurs became extinct 70 million years ....
(a) in   (b) before
(c) since   (d) ago

3. I'm just going to sleep .... two hours.
(a) for   (b) from
(c) till   (d) by

4. England has not won the World Cup in football .... 1966.
(a) in   (b) by
(c) at   (d) since

5. There is a meeting of all the office staff .... 2:30 sharp this afternoon.
(a) in   (b) for
(c) at   (d) before

6. My grandmother is always up .... dawn.
(a) for   (b) from
(c) till   (d) before

7. The Head Office of the company is open .... 9:30 AM to 6:00 PM, Monday to Friday.
(a) from   (b) for
(c) at   (d) to

Directions (Q. Nos. 8-12) Replace the underlined words with correct prepositions.

8. Many people stay on for the vigil <u>across</u> the midnight mass.
(a) between   (b) by
(c) after   (d) into

9. It took us a long time to find our way <u>into</u> the maze.
(a) over   (b) up
(c) through   (d) to

10. The boy is standing <u>under</u> the desk.
(a) after   (b) behind
(c) across   (d) on

11. You might get hurt if you jump <u>on</u> from that height.
(a) Down   (b) Out
(c) In   (d) Off

12. Ritu organised the cultural events in the college <u>since</u> her second year to the final year.
(a) For   (b) In
(c) From   (d) At

13. Improve the paragraph by changing its underlined portion.

The dromedary is a type of camel kept <u>to</u> desert people. It is not an easy animal to handle. It never becomes friends with its master or anybody else. Every night, these animals have to be pushed down to their knees and tied <u>onto</u> tightly. The dromedary is strong. It can easily throw off all it is carrying and gallop madly. To lead these animals, the nomads use long reins.

(a) by, up   (b) with, up
(c) at, over   (d) into, upon

Directions (Q. Nos. 14-18) Read the passage given below and fill in the blanks with suitable prepositions.

The rain had just stopped. I went .... into the garden. Then I heard a soft mewing. I saw a little white kitten. It was so thin that its bones were showing. It was wet and shivering. I brought it .... the house and dried it. My brother came .... "Do you know who this kitten belongs ....?" I asked him. My brother said he had seen some kittens .... the long grass .... our house. The mother cat was just a stray. He told me to give the kitten some fish. There was no more fish, so I took some rice and gave it to the kitten. But it would not eat the rice. "I wonder if it's old enough to eat rice."

14. The rain had just stopped. I went .... into the garden.
(a) from   (b) out   (c) onto   (d) over

15. It was wet and shivering. I brought it .... the house and dried it.
(a) in   (b) onto   (c) into   (d) near

16. My brother came ....
(a) in   (b) into
(c) over   (d) about

17. "Do you know who this kitten belongs ....?" I asked him.
(a) from   (b) to
(c) off   (d) over

18. My brother said he had seen some kittens .... the long grass .... our house.
(a) in, on   (b) near, in
(c) in, near   (d) off, near

2 Marks Questions

19. Improve the paragraph by changing its underlined portion.
Francis Macomber had half an hour before being carried <u>on</u> his tent from the edge of the camp <u>at</u> triumph. When the boys put him <u>up</u> at the door <u>from</u> his tent, he had shaken all their hands and received their congratulations.

(a) up, on, down, for   (b) to, in, up, for
(c) to, in, down, of   (d) up, on, up, of

20. Identify the sentence with a correct use of preposition.
(a) The bank is located in the end of this road.
(b) The company has opened an office on 41, Baker Street, London.
(c) The students are talking about the football match.
(d) The hotel is adjacent of the railway station.

21. Identify the sentence with an incorrect use of preposition.
    (a) Divide the pizza equally among the four of you.
    (b) The painting hangs on the wall.
    (c) Many people travel by local train everyday.
    (d) There is a lake in the fields.

22. Match the following to fill in the blanks with prepositions.

List-I	List-II
A. Upon	1. Why did you beat him .... a stick?
B. With	2. You can't leave a country .... a passport.
C. Without	3. The last date of income tax payment is almost .... us.
D. By	4. Bananas are sold .... the dozen.

Codes

	A	B	C	D
(a)	3	4	2	1
(b)	2	1	3	4
(c)	3	1	2	4
(d)	2	4	3	1

23. Identify the sentences with an incorrect use of compound prepositions.
    (a) The weather will be good this weekend according to Tom.
    (b) She is interested in anything concerning horses.
    (c) He picked up the penny from beneath the couch.
    (d) Tina is doing her homework with a pen.

24. Identify the sentences with a correct use of compound prepositions.
    (a) There is a friendly mouse inside my cupboard.
    (b) Amidst all the confusion, Saanvi stayed calm and saved the drowning kid.
    (c) My son emerged over the curtains to scare me.
    (d) My little brother collected my trophy on behalf of our sister.

25. Fill in the blanks with phrasal preposition from the option.
    1. There is rehabilitation centre .... my friend's office.
    2. I stand here .... you all to demonstrate my qualities as a great leader.

    Which of the following options can be used to fill in the blanks in both sentences?

    (a) in addition to   (b) on top of
    (c) in front of   (d) on account of

Chapter 08

Conjunctions

1 Mark Questions

Directions (Q. Nos. 1-6) Replace the underlined words with appropriate conjunctions.

1. The tire was flat; <u>however</u>, we called a service station.
   (a) Otherwise   (b) Therefore
   (c) Meanwhile   (d) Nevertheless

2. <u>And</u> Marge was late for work, she received a cut in pay.
   (a) So   (b) While
   (c) Although   (d) Because

3. I don't know <u>when</u> I can buy a pair of jeans.
   (a) Why   (b) And
   (c) But   (d) Where

4. He knew he was in the woods <u>but</u> he could hear the sound of some wolves howling.
   (a) As   (b) And
   (c) So   (d) Yet

5. Nitin was so excited that <u>but</u> his legs were aching, he began running.
   (a) Because   (b) Otherwise
   (c) Although   (d) Meanwhile

6. My friend said that the book was great, <u>for</u> I read it too.
   (a) Yet   (b) But
   (c) So   (d) Nor

Directions (Q. Nos 7-11) Fill in the blanks with suitable conjunctions.

7. She tells him he can get it himself .... do her a favour in the future by always getting it himself.
   (a) but   (b) and
   (c) yet   (d) either

8. All the precautions must have been neglected, ... the epidemic spread violently.
   (a) Either   (b) Yet
   (c) Unless   (d) For

9. The Fire brigade called in all their men .... they could douse the flames.
   (a) even if   (b) whereas
   (c) although   (d) so that

10. Last year, my sister .... won the 'Best in Academics' award, ... the 'Best in sports' award.
    (a) not, but
    (b) not only, but also
    (c) either, as
    (d) whether, or

11. Jaswant has very little money; ....
    his brother Satwant is a millionaire.
    (a) Hence   (b) Either
    (c) Conversely   (d) Finally

2 Marks Questions

12. Identify the sentence with the correct use of conjunctions.
    (a) Mohan couldn't tell his wife the truth also he lied.
    (b) He is a very weak President; otherwise most people support him.
    (c) Besides being clever, she is also very perceptive.
    (d) I don't know why Rohan came; consequently I would tell you.

13. Identify the sentence with an incorrect use of conjunctions.
    (a) He runs slowly as he is fat.
    (b) We had hoped to go to Spain; instead, we ended up in France.
    (c) I need to work hard so that I can pass the exam.
    (d) I don't know why I can buy a pair of jeans.

14. Choose the conjunctions that can be used to fill in both the blanks.
    1. I had .... a heavy breakfast .... I had to forego lunch.
    2. The man spoke with .... passion .... all the listeners were moved to tears.
    (a) no sooner, than
    (b) such, that
    (c) either, or
    (d) not only, but also

15. Read the passage and fill in the blanks with conjunctions from the options given below.
    Hummingbirds are small and colourful. Their legs are weak, ... their wings are strong. The wings beat fast and make a humming sound. They can hang in the air .... drink from a flower.
    (a) yet, but   (b) but, but
    (c) but, and   (d) and, yet

16. Which of the following sentences incorrectly uses conjunction?
    (a) The experiment's findings were groundbreaking. So, the scientists published a paper.
    (b) Until I get over my nausea, I will never be an astronaut.
    (c) Your dog got into my yard; however, he dug up my petunias.
    (d) She really wanted to eat ice cream; instead, she had a salad.

17. Which of the following sentences correctly uses conjunction?
    (a) I love the colour pink; nonetheless, this shade seems a little too light.
    (b) Would you rather go hiking on the coast but in the mountains?
    (c) I have to go to work at six, yet I'm waking up at four.
    (d) Whether only is dark chocolate delicious or it can be healthy.

18. Replace the underlined words with appropriate conjunctions.
    Sheila and Nancy are my sisters. Sheila likes to sing <u>for</u> Nancy enjoys knitting. Nancy dreams about cooking all day, <u>because</u> she has never ventured into the kitchen.
    (a) But, yet   (b) Yet, yet
    (c) Yet, and   (d) but, and

19. Fill in the blanks with appropriate conjunctions.
    I live in Sweden. I am still not familiar with most of the places .... I have been living here for long. I live in Sweden .... I got a job here almost ten years ago.
    (a) although, although
    (b) although, because
    (c) because, although
    (d) because, because

Tenses

1 Mark Questions

Directions (Q. Nos. 1-5) Read the following sentences and identify the tense used in them.

1. I had been working since morning.
(a) Past Progressive
(b) Past Perfect Progressive
(c) Past Perfect
(d) Simple Past

2. Have the students understood the problem clearly?
(a) Simple Present
(b) Present Progressive
(c) Present Perfect
(d) Present Perfect Progressive

3. Reena will be applying for MBA in one of the universities of Germany.
(a) Simple Future
(b) Future Progressive
(c) Future Perfect
(d) Future Perfect Progressive

4. I had not started my lunch before you came.
(a) Simple Past
(b) Past Progressive
(c) Past Perfect
(d) Past Perfect Progressive

5. Our country will have uprooted the problems of dowry and domestic violence by the end of this century.
(a) Simple Future
(b) Future Progressive
(c) Future Perfect
(d) Future Perfect Progressive

Directions (Q. Nos. 6-10) Fill in the blanks with appropriate form of the verbs.

6. I .... to visit you yesterday, but you .... not at home.
(a) wanted, were   (b) want, were
(c) will want, were (d) has wanted, were

7. The climate of the city .... mild and pleasant most of the time.
(a) is remaining   (b) remains
(c) is remained   (d) was remaining

8. The criminal .... the place before the police could reach.
(a) was escaping   (b) is escaping
(c) had escaped   (d) will escape

9. The runner .... the world record in Frankfurt. Two days later he .... even faster.
(a) break, run   (b) broke, ran
(c) had broke, run (d) will break, ran

10. Aryan .... his mother in making rangoli in the yard for last one hour.

    (a) is helping   (b) has helped

    (c) has been helping (d) helps

11. Fill in the blank with verb in future perfect tense.

    You can call me at work at 8 am. I ...... at the office by 8.

    (a) will have arrive (b) will had arrive

    (c) will had   (d) will have arrived

12. Fill in the blank with verb in past perfect continuous tense.

    He .... milk out of the carton when Mom walked into the kitchen.

    (a) had been drunk

    (b) was drinking

    (c) had been drinking

    (d) Will had been drinking

13. Which one of the following is an example of present perfect tense?

    (a) He has worked in New York since he left school.

    (b) Rohan has been playing since morning.

    (c) Are you listening to her properly?

    (d) Your ward has not been coming to school for last one week.

2 Marks Questions

14. Improve the paragraph by changing its underlined portion.

    It was a hot day, so I <u>decide</u> to prepare salad for lunch. Outside, the children <u>had playing</u> in the garden. Suddenly I <u>hear</u> a loud noise, followed by a scream. I <u>run</u> outside to see what <u>happened</u>.

    (a) Have decided, playing, have hear, happen

    (b) Decided, were playing, heard, ran, was happening

    (c) Will decide, was playing, heard, will run, has happened

    (d) Has decided, playing, hear, ran, happening

15. Choose the correct present continuous tense sentence from the options.

    (a) He have been reading this book for two hours.

    (b) She has been cooking since last night.

    (c) They have been waiting for you all day.

    (d) Are you having breakfast at this moment?

16. Choose the correct present continuous tense sentence from the options.

    (a) The boys were playing football after school.

    (b) She is constantly changing her hair colour.

    (c) The baby was crying before her father came.

    (d) She has been watching TV for six hours.

17. Choose the correct simple past tense sentence from the options.

    (a) A large trunk will come around the corner.

    (b) They had bought 2 tickets for the Rolling Stone concert.

    (c) We were playing basketball last Sunday.

    (d) Did they lose the match yesterday?

18. Match the following.

List-I (Types of Tense)		List-II (Examples)
A. Simple Past Tense	1.	He has been travelling around the world for a month.
B. Future Perfect Continuous Tense	2.	Yesterday, Alia had been reading the newspaper since 7 a.m.
C. Past Perfect Continuous Tense	3.	Jagruti will have been preparing her speech till afternoon tomorrow.
D. Present Perfect Continuous Tense	4.	They did not take their studies seriously.

Codes

	A	B	C	D		A	B	C	D
(a)	1	2	3	4	(b)	4	3	2	1
(c)	2	4	1	3	(d)	3	1	4	2

19. Change the given statement from present perfect tense to present perfect continuous tense. Choose the correct option.

They have stayed at the hotel since 9 o' clock.

(a) They have being stayed at the hotel since 9'o clock.

(b) The have staying at the hotel since 9 o'clock.

(c) They have been staying at the hotel since 9 o'clock.

(d) They has been staying at the hotel since 9 o'clock.

20. Choose the correct future perfect tense sentence from the options.

(a) Will you come to the party tomorrow?

(b) I will have been working all day tomorrow.

(c) Ram will not have done his work tomorrow.

(d) They will look after their son.

21. Change the given statement from simple past tense to past perfect tense. Choose from the options given below.

He completed the employee performance reviews last week.

(a) He had complete the employee performance reviews last week.

(b) He had been completing the employee performance reviews last week.

(c) He had completes the employee performance reviews last week.

(d) He had completed the employee performance reviews last week.

Active and Passive Voice

1 Mark Questions

Directions (Q. Nos. 1-6) From the options, choose the correct passive voice for the given sentences.

1. They make these tractors in Germany.
   (a) These tractors are being made in Germany.
   (b) These tractors are made in Germany.
   (c) These tractors were made in Germany.
   (d) These tractors have been made in Germany.

2. You must not drop garbage on the road.
   (a) Garbage must not be dropped on the road.
   (b) Garbage is not to be dropped on the road.
   (c) Garbage will not be dropped on the road.
   (d) Garbage is not supposed to be dropped on the road.

3. Someone broke my bedroom window last night.
   (a) My bedroom window was broken last night.
   (b) My bedroom window had been broken last night.
   (c) My bedroom window was being broken last night.
   (d) My bedroom window has been broken last night.

4. People will need public transport.
   (a) Public transport is needed.
   (b) Public transport was needed.
   (c) Public transport will be needed by people.
   (d) Public transport would be needed.

5. Somebody must have stolen my purse.
   (a) My purse is being stolen by somebody.
   (b) My purse must have been stolen by somebody.
   (c) My purse was stolen by somebody.
   (d) My purse may have been stolen by somebody.

6. Who had guided them to that place?
   (a) By whom has they been guided to that place?
   (b) By whom will they been guided to that place?
   (c) By whom had they been guided to that place?
   (d) By whom were they been guided to that place?

Directions (Q. Nos. 7-10) Fill in the blanks with suitable active or passive verb forms using the correct options.

7. The robbers .... by the police.
   (a) have arrested
   (b) have been arrested
   (c) was arrested
   (d) had arrested

8. We .... for the examinations.
   (a) have preparing
   (b) are preparing
   (c) had preparing
   (d) has been preparing

9. The students .... to submit their reports by the end of this week.
   (a) have been ask
   (b) were asked
   (c) has asked
   (d) are asking

10. The students .... by the teacher for stealing in the class.
    (a) has been punished
    (b) were being punished
    (c) were been punished
    (d) are punished

Directions (Q. Nos. 11-14) In this exercise, the first sentences are in the active voice. Fill in the blanks to say the same thing in passive voice.

11. They were interviewing her for the job.
    She .... for the job.
    (a) was being interviewed
    (b) was interviewed
    (c) has been interviewed
    (d) been interviewed

12. Tom is writing the letter.
    The letter .... by Tom.
    (a) is written   (b) is being written
    (c) was written   (d) was being written

13. Everyone understands English.
    English .... by everyone.
    (a) was understood
    (b) has been understood
    (c) is understood
    (d) is understand

14. The employees brought up this issue during the meeting.
    This issue .... by the employees during the meeting.
    (a) has been brought up
    (b) is brought up
    (c) was brought up
    (d) had been brought up

2 Marks Questions

15. Improve the sentences by changing them into active voice.
    The guests were being attended at the party last night by Kunal.
    (a) Kunal was attending the guests at the party last night.
    (b) Kunal had been attending the guests at the party last night.
    (c) The guests were being attended by Kunal at the party last night.
    (d) Kunal has been attending the guests at the party last night.

16. Consider the following statements.
    1. His blessing will be showered on us one day by God.
    2. God will have been showered his blessings on us one day.
    3. God will shower his blessings on us one day.

Which of the these is/are a grammatically correct sentence in active voice?

(a) 1 and 3   (b) Only 2

(c) Only 3   (d) 2 and 3

17. Match the following to complete a sentence in active voice.

List-I		List-II
A. The principal has forbidden	1.	book their tickets early.
B. We advice passengers to	2.	injured to the hospital.
C. The fireman took the	3.	in the rainy season.
D. Farmers sow maize	4.	smoking on the campus.

Codes

	A	B	C	D		A	B	C	D
(a)	1	4	3	2	(b)	4	1	2	3
(c)	3	1	4	2	(d)	2	3	1	4

18. Which of these sentences is in active voice?

(a) The gates had been opened by the gatekeeper.

(b) The message was given by Roshan yesterday.

(c) The car has been sold by my father.

(d) The old women were discussing the matter.

19. Which of these sentences is in passive voice?

(a) We decided to visit Spain, Portugal , Greece and Italy's mountains.

(b) I noticed that the window of that room had been left open by mistake.

(c) I need to call Sally, Tom, Peter and Crey for the party tomorrow.

(d) The poor man was carrying a torn bag.

Directions (Q. Nos. 20 and 21) Read the passage and fill in the blanks to form the passage in passive voice.

The Titanic was built in 1912. It was designed in a new way and was thought to be unsinkable. Because of this, it ....**20(i)**.... enough lifeboats. The hull ....**20(ii)**.... by a collision with a huge iceberg and it sank. A total of 1513 people ...**21(i)**.... that day. Several films ...**21(ii)**... about the ship since then.

20. (i) (a) wasn't give

(b) hadn't been given

(c) wasn't gave

(d) haven't been given

20. (ii) (a) was damaged

(b) had been damage

(c) was damage

(d) had damaged

21. (i) (a) was drowned

(b) were drown

(c) were drowned

(d) did drowned

21. (ii) (a) has made

(b) have been made

(c) have made

(d) has been make

Direct and Indirect Speech

1 Mark Questions

Directions (Q. Nos. 1-7) Change the direct speech into indirect speech by choosing the correct option.

1. Mohini said, "I visited my parents during the weekend."
   Mohini said that she .... her parents during the weekend.
   (a) has visited   (b) did visit
   (c) had visited   (d) visited

2. Girish said, "I didn't go to the party".
   Girish said that he .... to the party.
   (a) has not gone
   (b) had not gone
   (c) not went
   (d) will have not gone

3. Malini said, "I hadn't travelled by the Metro train before I came to Delhi".
   Malini said that she .... by the Metro train before she .... to Delhi.
   (a) did not travel, came
   (b) hadn't travelled, had came
   (c) hadn't travelled, came
   (d) never travelled, had come

4. She said, "He hasn't eaten breakfast."
   She said/informed that he .... breakfast.
   (a) didn't eat   (b) hadn't eaten
   (c) haven't eaten   (d) will not have eaten

5. Jiten said, "I will eat pizza for dinner."
   Jiten said that he .... pizza for dinner.
   (a) will eat   (b) will be eating
   (c) would eat   (d) is going to eat

6. Raveena said, "I'm coming, wait for me"!
   Raveena exclaimed that we should wait for her, as she ....
   (a) is coming
   (b) was coming
   (c) has been coming
   (d) had been coming

7. Deepika said, "I was sleeping when Priya called."
   Deepika said that she .... when Priya called.
   (a) was sleeping
   (b) has been sleeping
   (c) had been sleeping
   (d) were sleeping

Directions (Q. Nos. 8-14) Change the indirect speech into direct speech by choosing the correct option.

8. He told me that I might leave that place as soon as I could.
   He said to me, ''You .... this place as soon as ....''
   (a) should leave, you should
   (b) may leave, you can
   (c) will leave, you would
   (d) may leave, you could

9. I admitted that I had acted foolishly in what I said.
   I said, "I .... foolishly in what I said."
   (a) have acted   (b) has acted
   (c) act   (d) had been acted

10. He told them that he had been robbed of the book which he had brought.
    He said," I .... of the book which I ...."
    (a) have been robbed, bought
    (b) has been robbed, buy
    (c) had been robbed, buy
    (d) had been robbed, had bought

11. He said that he was sorry for the fault he had committed.
    He said,"I .... for the fault I .... "
    (a) am sorry, have committed
    (b) was sorry, had committed
    (c) will be sorry, had committed
    (d) am sorry, had committed

12. They affirmed that he was the best worker they had seen.
    They said, "He .... worker we ...."
    (a) are, had seen
    (b) is the best, have seen
    (c) is the best, has seen
    (d) is the best, had seen

13. He made a promise that he would do it as soon as he could.
    He made a promise, "I .... as soon as I ...."
    (a) shall do it, could
    (b) will do it, could
    (c) will do it, can
    (d) would do it, can

14. They said that he had deserved their thanks for all he had done.
    They said,"He .... our thanks for all he has done."
    (a) has deserved
    (b) had deserved
    (c) will deserve
    (d) deserved

Directions (Q. Nos. 15-17) Read the dialogues given below and then complete the reported speech by choosing the correct option.

Ajay : "What are you doing here Asha? I haven't seen you since April."
Asha : "I've just come back from my two months long holiday in Kashmir."
Ajay : "Did you enjoy it?"
Asha : "I love Kashmir. And the Kashmiri people were so friendly."

Dialogues in Reported Speech

Ajay asked Asha ....**(15)**......... . He further added that he hadn't seen her since April. Asha explained that ....**(16)**......... . Ajay wondered if she had enjoyed it. Asha told him that she ....**(17)**........, and that the Kashmiri people had been so friendly.

Options

15. (a) what she was doing there
    (b) what was she doing there
    (c) what she has been doing there
    (d) what she had been doing there

16. (a) she has just come back from her two months long holiday in Kashmir

(b) she had just come back from her two months long holiday in Kashmir

(c) she just came back from her two months long holiday in Kashmir

(d) she was coming back from her two months long holiday in Kashmir

17. (a) loves Kashmir

(b) loved Kashmir

(c) has loved Kashmir

(d) had loved Kashmir

2 Marks Questions

18. Fill in the blanks correctly to make a proper sentence in indirect form.

Prabha said that she had .... to the shopping centre when the thief .... open the lock, ... her house and stole the precious and antique timepiece.

(a) Went, break, enter

(b) Gone, broken, have entered

(c) Gone, broke, entered

(d) Is going, was broken, had entered

19. Choose the sentence that shows the correct use of reported speech.

(a) He says that he would buy a new house, if he have been rich.

(b) My sister said that she had already eaten her piece of cake.

(c) My son say that he often have a big hamburger.

(d) Dentist said that my father need an operation.

20. Match the following to complete a sentence in direct speech.

	List-I		List-II
A.	"Don't worry about the tickets,	1.	At that horse shaped cloud."
B.	Nia said, "It's so noisy, I cannot	2.	I'll pay for them," said Jack.
C.	The child exclaimed in joy, "Look	3.	Be fine," said the doctor.
D.	"Don't worry about Nickil, he'll	4.	Concentrate, can you?"

Codes

	A	B	C	D
(a)	3	1	2	4
(b)	1	4	2	3
(c)	2	4	1	3
(d)	3	2	4	1

21. Match the following.

	List-I (Direct speech)		List-II (Indirect Speech)
A.	Last night	1.	The day before
B.	Today	2.	The night before
C.	Yesterday	3.	That day
D.	Tomorrow	4.	The next day

Codes

	A	B	C	D
(a)	1	2	3	4
(b)	2	3	1	4
(C)	3	1	4	2
(d)	2	1	3	4

22. Choose the sentence that shows the correct use of direct speech.

(a) The Minister say "There will be being no growth this year."

(b) Go to bed! Mother said to the children.

(c) To teacher says, "Did you did your homework?"

(d) "I will be using the car myself on the 31st", she said.

Chapter 12

Error Detection

1 Mark Questions

Directions (Q. Nos. 1-14) Each sentence has been divided into four parts, namely A, B, C and D. One of these parts carries a mistake, which may be a grammatical, punctuation or spelling mistake. Select the part which carries the mistake.

1. She was conscious to all that was going on around her house.
   A / B / C / D

2. Sarla is grateful of her uncle for the moral and material support on his part to enable her
   A / B / C
   to continue her higher studies.
   D

3. We use to go to the college ground every evening to play football.
   A / B / C / D

4. There were long queues on the booking windows of cinema halls on the eve of Holi.
   A / B / C / D

5. Mohan was taken with surprise to see Harish wearing a new uniform.
   A / B / C / D

6. The flood has taken a toll of more than a hundred lives in Kashmir and has
   A / B / C
   made much havoc there.
   D

7. If you was not conversant with the work, how can you do even your routine
   A / B / C
   office work in that department?
   D

8. The US sponsored move to boycott the Moscow Olympics failed in spite of the massive
   A / B / C
   propaganda of their part.
   D

9. The prospect of peace between Iraq and the ISIS rebels are not so bright
       A   B   C

                       as the danger of further escalation of the war.
                                      D

10. The number of trains on almost all the important routes have been increased,
     A   B   C

                          but every train goes packed.
                             D

11. The dictionary, as well as the textbook, were missing from the room.
      A   B   C   D

12. The price of onions is going up in the open market because there is not enough stock
     A   B   C

                    of the vegetable for everybody.
                        D

13. What do you think for the person I had recommended for a job in your office?
       A   B   C   D

14. Our school requires every student to bring there own instrument box
      A   B   C

                   for the geometric drawing classes.
                         D

Directions (Q. Nos. 15-21) Underlined parts (A, B, C and D) of the given sentences may contain an error in grammar usage, diction or idiom. Select the part that is incorrect.

15. It must(A) be him(B) with whom(C) you enjoy to do(D) your project.

16. Competence(A) without willingness(B) yields(C) in(D) a half-hearted result.

17. Tagore's ability to summarise(A) the range of(B) human emotions in simple yet profound(C) eloquent verse is perhaps the greatest reason for his enduring(D) popularity.

18. Determination(A) of the long term effects(B) of CFCs on the upper atmosphere are(C) currently one of the most challenging(D) problems in climate research.

19. Since we were caught completely unaware(A), the affect(B) of the Director's remark was startling(C): some were shocked, but(D) others were angry.

20. We were terrified (A) by sounds: the screaming of (B) the wind, the restless rustled (C) of the leaves in the trees; and the sudden overwhelming (D) explosions of thunder.

21. She managed to enter (A) her house, bolted the door (B) from inside and slump on (D) the sofa.

2 Marks Questions

22. A sentence is given in four parts. One of the parts contains a grammatical error. Find the part.

A captain is a group member which (P) exerts profound influence (Q) on the behaviour and attitude of (R) other members of the team (S).

(a) Q   (b) S   (c) P   (d) R

23. Consider the following statements.

1. I go to visit my friend who lives in Gangtok, will you go there with me?
2. No, I don't think I should go there as I am not familiar with your friend.

Which of the these statement has a grammatical error?

(a) Only 1   (b) Only 2
(c) Both 1 and 2   (d) None of these

24. Choose the sentence that is without any grammatical error.

(a) She walking briskly meant that she was in a great hurry.
(b) Her walking briskly meant that she was in great hurry.
(c) Her brisk walk meant that her was in great hurry.
(d) She walked briskly and it means that was in great hurry.

25. State true or false where T is for grammatically correct and F is for error.

1. The car was not moving swiftly as it stopped frequently at regularly intervals.
2. People are believing in the medicines that the government dispensaries had provided.

(a) 1-T, 2-F   (b) 2-F, 2-T
(c) 1-T, 2-T   (d) 1-F, 2-F

26. Spot the error in the given sentence –

That queer looking woman that had kidnapped the rich business man's only son has now been apprehended and is being held in the city's prison.

  A. Woman that had
  B. Kidnapped the rich
  C. Been apprehended and
  D. Is held in the

Codes
(a) Only A
(b) A and B
(c) B and D
(d) Only C

27. Match the following to form complete sentences.

	List-I		List-II
A.	I don't know why so many people favor	1.	of very fine quality pashmina wool.
B.	This white embroidered shawl is made up	2.	have adverse effects on small shops.
C.	The arrival of branded supermarkets might	3.	about introduction of foreign goods.
D.	Time and again there have been concerns	4.	international brands instead of Indian.

Codes

	A	B	C	D
(a)	1	4	3	2
(b)	4	1	2	3
(c)	3	1	4	2
(d)	2	3	1	4

Sentence Arrangement

1 Mark Questions

Directions (Q. Nos. 1-8) Arrange the parts (P, Q, R) of the sentences to make meaningful sentences.

1. She faced the
   P. courage and managed to solve the
   Q. problem all by herself
   R. whole trouble with
   (a) PQR   (b) RQP   (c) QPR   (d) RPQ

2. As soon
   P. its master, it
   Q. as the dog saw
   R. started wagging its tail
   (a) PRQ   (b) QPR   (c) RPQ   (d) QRP

3. We saw a
   P. on the life of
   Q. the late President of South Africa, Nelson Mandela
   R. film which was based
   (a) QPR   (b) RPQ   (c) PRQ   (d) QRP

4. The new rug
   P. in the living room
   Q. not match the furniture
   R. is beautiful, but it does
   (a) QPR   (b) PQR
   (c) RPQ   (d) PRQ

5. Even though she
   P. studied hard because she
   Q. suffered from arthritis, she
   R. wanted to go to a medical school in London
   (a) QPR   (b) PQR
   (c) QRP   (d) PRQ

6. Because Alex and Michael
   P. before noon, I did not
   Q. see them at the station
   R. arrived at the bus station
   (a) QPR   (b) RPQ
   (c) PRQ   (d) QRP

7. Bobby was delighted he got a
   P. part was a small one
   Q. part in the school
   R. play, even though the
   (a) QRP   (b) PRQ
   (c) QPR   (d) PQR

8. What writers struggle to
   P. newspaper columns, the cartoon
   Q. manages in a pointed one-liner
   R. express through numerous
   (a) QRP   (b) QPR
   (c) RQP   (d) RPQ

Directions (Q. Nos. 9-14) Given below are five parts of a sentence. The first part (A) and the last part (Z) are given. Choose the order in which the three parts (P, Q, R) should appear in order to form a meaningful sentence.

9. A. With his unique style and
   P. had the audience swooning with fright and
   Q. God-gifted wit, he produced and
   R. directed some of the most thrilling films that
   Z. falling off their seats with laughter.
   (a) RPQ   (b) QRP   (c) RQP   (d) PQR

10. A. I've learned that
    P. but people will never forget
    Q. people will forget what you
    R. said, people will forget what you did
    Z. how you made them feel.
    (a) QPR   (b) QRP   (c) RQP   (d) RPQ

11. A. Ann Davidson, the first woman to sail
    P. was all set to begin her journey of
    Q. single-handedly to the Atlantic ocean,
    R. hopes, aspirations and journey of troubles,
    Z. when she received a gift pack.
    (a) RPQ   (b) QPR
    (c) PQR   (d) QRP

12. A. There is general
    P. as its most
    Q. concurrence that the pursuit of
    R. planning is seldom as successful
    Z. ardent advocates would like.
    (a) RQP   (b) QPR
    (c) QRP   (d) RPQ

13. A. The famous
    P. Kakori train robbery was
    Q. objective of getting money for carrying
    R. conceived with the sole
    Z. out their revolutionary activities.
    (a) QRP   (b) PQR
    (c) PRQ   (d) QPR

14. A. Prior to powering up
    P. back panel of the CPU and
    Q. the power cord is firmly connected to the
    R. the computer system, make sure that
    Z. is plugged into the wall socket.
    (a) QPR   (b) RPQ
    (c) RQP   (d) QRP

2 Marks Questions

Directions (Q. Nos. 15-20) In each of the following questions, a passage is given with the first and the last sentences identified as A and Z. The remaining four sentences are labeled as P, Q, R and S. Find the correct sequence of these four sentences and select the correct option accordingly.

15. A. Water is the most important liquid for all living forms.
    P. Water is available in 3 states on the Earth- solid, liquid and gaseous.
    Q. Solid-state includes glaciers, snow caps, ice sheets, and polar ice reserves.
    R. It is not only necessary for our life processes but is also required for the functioning of our planet.
    S. The liquid state includes rivers, seas, lakes, ponds, streams, oceans, and geysers.
    Z. The gaseous state includes water vapor found in the atmosphere.
    (a) RPQS   (b) PRQS
    (c) QPRS   (d) SQRP

16. A. Democracy is very important for human development.

P. Moreover, we have seen how other forms of government have turned out to be.

Q. When people have free will to live freely, they will be happier.

R. Citizens are not that happy and prosperous in a monarchy or anarchy.

S. Furthermore, democracy lets people have equal rights.

Z. This ensures that equality prevails all over the country.

(a) PQSR   (b) SPQR

(c) RSPQ   (d) QPRS

17. A. Nails provide vital clues to the state of your health.

P. A dysfunction in the lung, for instance, can be signalled by a bluish tinge to the nails.

Q. Yellowed nails, on the other hand, are a telltale sign of liver problems.

R. Heart disease is often revealed by reddish nails with white half moons.

S. The colour of the nails can act as an indicator of a general health problem.

Z. Although nails can highlight serious illness, they are far more likely to show up nutritional or vitamin and mineral deficiencies.

(a) RQPS   (b) SPRQ

(c) PRQS   (d) QPRS

18. A. Rudyard Kipling was a versatile writer with an articulate style of writing.

P. Kipling was the first English language writer to receive Nobel Prize for Literature.

Q. On one hand, his writings depicted an aureate style of writing.

R. He was an English short story writer, poet and novelist.

S. Whereas, on the other hand, his works have also shown careless and colloquial styles.

Z. Kipling was a versatile personality and had many qualities that made him extremely popular.

(a) QSRP   (b) RPQS

(c) SRQP   (d) PQSR

19. A. A panther was terrorising the Khulna district of Bangladesh, just outside the Sundarbans.

P. And it was growing bolder.

Q. It had recently carried off a little girl.

R. The previous victim was a man who had been attacked in broad daylight in his field.

S. She was the seventh person killed in two months by the animal.

Z. The beast dragged him off into the forest and his corpse was later found hanging from a tree.

(a) RSPQ   (b) SRQP

(c) PSRQ   (d) QSPR

20. A. Gautam Buddha was the founder of the Buddhism religion.

P. He was born in the ruling house of Kapilvastu, at Lumbini located at the foothills of Nepal in 566 B.C.

Q. His father's name was Suddhodhana.

R. He was a Chief of the Shakya Republic.

S. His mother, Mahamaya died, when he was only seven days old.

Z. Gautam Buddha was known by the name of "Siddhartha" in his childhood.

(a) PQRS   (b) QPSR

(c) SQPR   (d) RQPS

Chapter 14

Fillers

1 Mark Questions

Directions (Q. Nos. 1-15) Fill in each blank with the most suitable word.

The word 'Capsicum', originally from Central America, is the botanical name ....(1)....... a range of fruits (technically it is a fruit) ....(2)....... includes chillies, bell peppers and long banana peppers. ....(3)....... Singapore, the name 'capsicum' is used. In the USA ....(4)....... UK, the fruit is called 'bell pepper' ....(5)....... just 'pepper'. ......(6)....... versatile (can be eaten raw or cooked) fruits come in all shapes and sizes. In terms ....(7)....... colour, capsicums range ......(8)........ green capsicums that turn red ....(9)....... they ripen, to ....(10)....... medley of orange, yellow, purple and black shades. Whatever ......(11)........ shape or colour, the bigger the fruit, the sweeter the taste; the smaller ....(12)....... fruit, the spicier ....(13)....... is. When choosing capsicums, go for ......(14)........ with glossy skins. Avoid the ones ....(15)....... soft spots or blemishes.

1. (a) a   (b) and   (c) as   (d) for
2. (a) that   (b) for   (c) as   (d) or
3. (a) a   (b) in   (c) as   (d) for
4. (a) a   (b) and   (c) as   (d) for
5. (a) as   (b) and   (c) or   (d) for
6. (a) the   (b) and   (c) with   (d) these
7. (a) of   (b) the   (c) and   (d) for
8. (a) from   (b) and   (c) as   (d) for
9. (a) in   (b) and   (c) as   (d) for
10. (a) in   (b) it   (c) a   (d) for
11. (a) in   (b) it   (c) a   (d) its
12. (a) in   (b) the   (c) that   (d) with
13. (a) in   (b) it   (c) a   (d) for
14. (a) these   (b) with   (c) of   (d) those
15. (a) with   (b) from   (c) that   (d) these

2 Marks Questions

Directions (Q. Nos. 16-20) Read the following passage and fill in the blanks.

Do the voters vote for their favourite candidates by making ......(16)......... decisions? Or are they taking rational decisions? Do people find enough time to vote for their favourite candidate on the basis of ....(17)....... i.e. by considering the candidate's policies, his vision etc. or are they finding shortcut ways to select a particular candidate based on their first ....(18)........? These are some of the questions that snag my mind.

Through a ......(19)......... of various research projects; the writer says why the voters vote for a candidate. The basic idea that the article talks about is that political decisions are based upon one's ....(20)........ appearance.

16. (a) immediate   (b) intuitive   (c) instinct   (d) natural

17. (a) reasoning   (b) rational   (c) rationale   (d) validation

18. (a) speeches   (b) aggressions   (c) parody   (d) impressions

19. (a) compendium   (b) concise   (c) contentions   (d) assortment

20. (a) own   (b) physical   (c) competitive   (d) mental

Directions (Q. Nos. 21-25) This is an excerpt from 'Call of the Wild' by Jack London. Read the passage and fill in the blanks.

He was glad for one thing: the rope was off his neck. That ....(21)........ them an unfair advantage; but now that it was off, he would show them. They would never get another rope around his neck. Upon that he ....(22)......... . For two days and nights he neither ate nor ......(23)......... . During those two days of ....(24)......., he accumulated enough courage and planning to devise his escape route. His eyes turned blood shot due to rage, his whole body ached severely but his mind was bent upon to materialise his ....(25)........ plan of freedom.

21. (a) have given   (b) gave   (c) had given   (d) would be giving

22. (a) was resolved   (b) were resolved   (c) has to be resolved   (d) could be resolved

23. (a) drunk nothing   (b) drank anything   (c) dring something   (d) drank

24. (a) peril   (b) havoc   (c) turmoil   (d) torment

25. (a) premeditated   (b) intentional   (c) impractical   (d) meticulous

Chapter 15

Synonyms and Antonyms

1 Mark Questions

Synonyms

Choose the synonyms of the underlined word.

1. Many of us have <u>ambivalent</u> feelings about our politicians, admiring but also distrusting them.
   (a) approving   (b) critical
   (c) disturbing   (d) mixed

2. Some animals like the giant land tortoise have remarkable <u>longevity</u>, as they can live several hundred years.
   (a) age duration   (b) appearance
   (c) habits   (d) body length

3. The family lived a very simple life with no need for <u>extravagant</u> purchases.
   (a) Thrifty   (b) Modest
   (c) Expensive   (d) Calm

4. Some mentally ill people have <u>bizarre</u> ideas like thinking that the TV is talking to them or that others can steal their thoughts.
   (a) limited   (b) strange
   (c) ordinary   (d) brilliant

5. <u>Nocturnal</u> creatures such as bats and owls have highly developed senses that enable them to function in the dark.
   (a) feathery
   (b) brainy
   (c) night time
   (d) living

Antonyms

Choose the Antonyms of the underlined word.

6. A former employee of the company, <u>irate</u> over having been fired, barged into their factory and damaged some costly machines.
   (a) undecided
   (b) livid
   (c) calm
   (d) indignant

7. The car wash we organised to raise funds for our workshop was a <u>fiasco</u>, as it rained all day.
   (a) success
   (b) surprise
   (c) mess
   (d) disaster

8. "My doctor said that smoking could <u>terminate</u> my life. But I told him, "Everybody's life has to end sometime."
   (a) extremity   (b) begin
   (c) climax   (d) call off

9. As soon as I made a <u>flippant</u> remark to my boss, I regretted sounding so disrespectful.
   (a) serious
   (b) idiotic
   (c) disrespectful
   (d) useful

10. Many people have pointed out the harmful effects that a working mother may have on the family, yet there are many <u>salutary</u> effects as well.
(a) irrelevant   (b) hurtful
(c) well-known   (d) healthy

11. During their training, police officers must respond to <u>simulated</u> emergencies in preparation for dealing with real ones.
(a) mild   (b) actual
(c) bogus   (d) made up

2 Marks Questions

12. Read the two sentences given below. Words are underlined in each sentence. Choose the synonym of both the words from the given options.
   I. Sam was not exactly <u>good-looking</u> but definitely attractive.
  II. His movements were <u>graceful</u> and elegant.
(a) Beautiful   (b) Incompetent
(c) Crummy   (d) Hideous

13. Choose the group of antonyms for the underlined word.
Ms. Samara translated the <u>fascinating</u> fairy tale into plain English.
(a) Fascinating, Absorbing, Amusing
(b) Boring, Dull, Monotonous
(c) Gripping, Tedious, Enthralling
(d) Repetitive, Unvaried, Interesting

14. Fill in the blanks using a pair of antonyms.
   I. We filled the blue pail with the .... marbles and the red pail with the .... marbles.
  II. He said he still found delight in all battles, ... and ....
(a) big, small   (b) short, long
(c) short, tall   (d) big, slow

15. Choose the antonym for words underlined in each sentence.
   I. My friend from school was <u>agreeable</u> and I have never seen him sad.
  II. I always try to make my lessons <u>enjoyable</u>.

(a) Unpleasant   (b) Sociable
(c) Attractive   (d) Pleasing

16. State True or False for the following statements, T stands for True and F stands for False.
  1. The synonyms of 'turmoil' can be confusion, chaos, mayhem, tumult and disorder.
  2. The antonym of 'initiative' can be laziness, cowardice, inventiveness and creativity.
(a) 1-T, 2-F   (b) 1-F, 2-T
(c) 1-F, 2-F   (d) 1-T, 2-T

17. Match the following synonyms.

List-I		List-II	
A.	Fleece	1.	Polished
B.	Suave	2.	Enthrall
C.	Captivate	3.	Sensible
D.	Prudent	4.	Swindle

Codes

	A	B	C	D		A	B	C	D
(a)	1	4	3	2	(b)	4	1	2	3
(c)	3	1	4	2	(d)	2	3	1	4

18. Match the following antonyms.

List-I		List-II	
A.	Lucrative	1.	Peaceful
B.	Aggressive	2.	Believable
C.	Tenacious	3.	Unprofitable
D.	Astounding	4.	Weak

Codes

	A	B	C	D		A	B	C	D
(a)	1	4	3	2	(b)	4	1	2	3
(c)	3	1	4	2	(d)	2	3	1	4

Chapter 16

Idioms and Phrases

1 Mark Questions

Directions (Q. Nos. 1-5) Choose the correct option to complete the idioms/ phrases.

1. God's mill grinds slow ....
   (a) but sure   (b) but always
   (c) but eventually   (d) but sometimes

2. A rolling stone ....
   (a) gathers no sauce
   (b) goes to the right hand
   (c) gathers no moss
   (d) falls in the well

3. A chain is only as strong as ....
   (a) its unknown link
   (b) its weakest link
   (c) it is held
   (d) it can be made

4. A fool and his money are ....
   (a) are not known   (b) soon finished
   (c) soon spent   (d) soon parted

5. Keep one's fingers ....
   (a) open   (b) crossed
   (c) closed   (d) tight

Directions (Q. Nos. 6-10) Fill in the blanks with the idioms/ phrases.

6. His bread is buttered ....
   (a) from the edge   (b) on one side
   (c) on the other side (d) on both sides

7. .... , he remained home.
   (a) While he was not well
   (b) As he was sick
   (c) Might he was sick
   (d) He was not well so

8. The newly wed couple painted the town .... with their extravagance.
   (a) red   (b) blue
   (c) yellow   (d) golden

9. She .... by interfering in her neighbour's affairs.
   (a) burnt her hand (b) saved herself
   (c) burnt her fingers (d) disclose herself

10. Today is my son's birthday, he is in ....
    (a) very happy mood
    (b) high spirits
    (c) great joy
    (d) a cheerful mood

Directions (Q. Nos. 11-13) Mark the option that is closest to the meaning of the given idioms/proverbs/phrases.

11. Jack was so confused; I gave him a <u>piece of my mind</u>.
    (a) Suggested him what to do
    (b) Agreed with what he said
    (c) Angrily expressed your opinion
    (d) Taught him a lesson

12. Although Nancy has studied French in her school, she knows it <u>after a fashion</u>.

(a) Thorough knowledge

(b) To a certain extent but not perfectly

(c) In depth information

(d) Surprising thing

13. Mr. Sudhir is not a successful lawyer but he has the <u>gift of the gab</u>.

(a) Ready to act on slight provocation

(b) Gift of finding the truth

(c) A talent for speaking

(d) None of the above

2 Marks Questions

14. Correct the statements by replacing the phrasal verbs in underline with the correct phrasal verbs.

1. He <u>backed into</u> two days before the holiday so we gave his ticket to his sister.

2. I was just <u>passing away</u> when I saw the accident.

(a) 1-backed out, 2-passing by

(b) 1-backed off, 2-passing back

(c) 1-back out, 2-pass by

(d) 1-back off, 2-pass back

15. Consider the following statements.

1. Do you think he will stop taking bribe after being caught and punished? I don't think so, **a leopard doesn't change its spots.**

2. Let's just **cross the stream where it is shallowest** and park our vehicle wherever we find a spot in this crowded parking plot.

Which of these statements show the correct use of the proverbs in bold?

(a) Only 1   (b) Only 2

(c) Both 1 and 2   (d) None of these

16. State true or false where T stands for correct use of idiom and F stands for incorrect use of idiom.

1. My daughter took away my breath when she came running to me with a trophy in her one hand and a silver medal on the other.

2. The doctor advised the patient to go for a CT scan immediately but he turned a deaf ear to the doctor's advice.

(a) 1-T, 2-F

(b) 1-T, 2-T

(c) 1-F, 2-T

(d) 1-F, 2-F

17. Fill in the blank the meaning of the phrasal verb (in bold) given in the first sentence.

The racing car **blew up** rapidly after it crashed into a fence just near the racing track.

Her head felt ready to .... with anger, and adrenaline warmed her from the inside out.

(a) explode

(b) rage

(c) go insane

(d) damage

18. Choose the correct option to complete the sentence that has a phrasal verb and an idiom.

The manager said to John, "Stop complaining and .... on with your work! This is your last warning. If you can't do your job properly, you're going to .... the sack."

(a) get, got

(b) got, get

(c) get, get

(d) got, got

19. Correct the statements by replacing the idioms in underline with the correct idioms.

1. We are pleased <u>high and low</u> with our new penthouse, but we have remodeled the kitchen and the terrace area.
2. Nitin searched <u>here and there</u> for the files but couldn't find them anywhere in his house.

(a) 1-Rough and ready, 2-sweetness and light
(b) 1-by and large, 2- high and low
(c) 1- still and all, 2-now and again
(d) 1-well and good,2-skin and bones

20. Consider the following statements.

1. We did what we could and now the <u>ball is in your court</u>.
2. I find the whole issue about these gender roles a <u>sweep under the rug</u>.
3. Mike saw his going to work for his father as a <u>necessary evil</u> if he was ever to own his own company sameday.

Which of these statements show the correct use of the underlined idioms?

(a) 1 and 2   (b) Only 1
(c) 1 and 3   (d) 2 and 3

21. Match the following.

List-I (Idioms)	List-II (Meanings)
A. My married daughter visits me off and on.	1. Deeply affected
B. She took to heart, the death of her husband.	2. Consider
C. He should take into account his past services.	3. Available
D. My parents are always on hand if we need a babysitter.	4. Occasionally

Codes

	A	B	C	D
(a)	1	4	3	2
(b)	4	1	2	3
(c)	3	1	4	2
(d)	2	3	1	4

22. Match the following to fill the blanks with the correct idioms/phrase.

List-I	List-II
A. I can make .... of the story told by him.	1. Icing on a cake
B. India's win over Pakistan on Independence day was like	2. Put a screw on
C. Wherever I see indiscipline , I cannot tolerate and	3. Neither head nor tail
D. His teacher .... him to vote for his brother.	4. Put my foot down

Codes

	A	B	C	D		A	B	C	D
(a)	1	4	3	2	(b)	4	1	2	3
(c)	3	1	4	2	(d)	2	3	1	4

One Word Substitution

1 Mark Questions

Directions (Q. Nos. 1-5) Choose one word for the given definitions.

1. A person who does not believe in the existence of God.
   (a) Theist   (b) Pessimist
   (c) Atheist   (d) Agnostic

2. A person who sacrifices his life for a cause.
   (a) Martyr   (b) Patriot
   (c) Compassionate (d) Emphatic

3. A fixed orbit in space in relation to the planet Earth.
   (a) Geo-positioning (b) Geo-synchronous
   (c) Geo-stationary (d) Stationary

4. One who knows everything.
   (a) Omnivore   (b) Omniscient
   (c) Omni verse   (d) Omnipotent

5. A narrow piece of land connecting two big landmasses.
   (a) Strait   (b) Peninsula
   (c) Estuary   (d) Isthmus

Directions (Q. Nos. 6-10) Choose the correct option for the given professions.

6. A person who studies about ancient things.
   (a) Anthropologist (b) Historian
   (c) Archaeologist (d) Philosopher

7. A person that patrols the area to see that vehicles are parked at proper place.
   (a) Traffic controller
   (b) Traffic warden
   (c) Traffic police
   (d) All of the above

8. A person who introduces the contestants in a stage show.
   (a) Compere   (b) Speaker
   (c) Introducer   (d) Calligrapher

9. A person who conducts an art dealing or care takes the museum collections.
   (a) Curator   (b) Collector
   (c) Art dealer   (d) Ethnographer

10. One who studies the elections and trends of voting.
    (a) Cartographer   (b) Psephologist
    (c) Orator   (d) Pathologist

Directions (Q. Nos. 11-15) Choose the correct option for the given definitions.

11. The commencement of words with the same letter usually seen in poetry.
    (a) Metaphor   (b) Oxymoron
    (c) Alliteration   (d) Irony

12. A collection of wild animals kept in captivity for exhibition.
    (a) Menagerie   (b) Infirmary
    (c) Aviary   (d) Apiary

13. An image or write up that can be interpreted to reveal a hidden meaning as moral or satire.

(a) Archives   (b) Ephemeral
(c) Arsenal   (d) Allegory

14. A country or a state run by the worst, least qualified or most unscrupulous people.

(a) Democracy   (b) Kakistocracy
(c) Neocracy   (d) Oligarchy

15. An extreme or irrational fear of the darkness or the night.

(a) Nyctophobia   (b) Logophobia
(c) Pharmacophobia (d) Autophobia

Directions (Q. Nos. 16-20) In questions given below fill in the blanks with the correct alternative.

16. Hitler was known notoriously for the .... he committed against the Jewish community.

(a) homicide   (b) infanticide
(c) genocide   (d) filicide

17. In the famous fairy tale, Cinderella, she was a .... maid.

(a) honorary   (b) scullery
(c) tannery   (d) creche

18. This time the cotton harvest was good and 200 .... were produced.

(a) bales   (b) pieces
(c) yarns   (d) textiles

19. My tutor is a sort of ...., she speaks seven different languages.

(a) recluse   (b) steward
(c) polyglot   (d) stoic

20. The use of fingers and hands to convey your idea is called ....

(a) odontology
(b) dactylology
(c) psychology
(d) chronobiology

2 Marks Questions

21. Choose the incorrect option.

A. A strong or/and fast moving stream of water or any other liquid- torrent.
B. A secret or disguised way of writing to maintain secrecy such as a coded message- cypher.
C. A Christian community where nuns live together under monastic vows – monastery.
D. Study of the law of the flow of water and other liquids – hydraulics

Codes

(a) Only A   (b) Both C and D
(c) Only C   (d) Both A and B

22. Choose the option which correctly substitutes the given phrase.

1. A piece of enclosed land planted with fruit trees: Orchard.
2. A large natural or artificial lake used as a source of water supply: Oasis

(a) Only 1   (b) Only 2
(c) Both 1 and 2   (d) None of these

23. State True or False for the following statements, T stands for True and F stands for False.

1. A type of government that is not connected with any type of religious or spiritual matters is called socialist type of government.
2. A style of government where the representatives are elected by the entire population or all the eligible members of a state is called autonomy.

(a) 1-T, 2-F   (b) 1-F, 2-T
(c) 1-F, 2-F   (d) 1-T, 2-T

24. Match the following.

	List-I		List-II
A.	The doctor who treats heart diseases	1.	Pedagogy
B.	A sound that cannot be heard	2.	Cardiologist
C.	A thing that is kept as a reminder of a person, place or event	3.	Souvenir
D.	The method and practice of teaching	4.	Inaudible

Codes

	A	B	C	D
(a)	2	4	3	1
(b)	4	1	2	3
(c)	3	1	4	2
(d)	2	3	1	4

25. Replace the underline words by the most suitable word to make a proper sentence.

The best season for transplanting of the <u>trees whose leaves fall in the autumn</u> is the month of October,November as the soil is dry but not too dry like in summers.

(a) Tropical   (b) Alpine

(c) Deciduous   (d) Himalayan

26. Match the following words with their meanings.

	List-I		List-II
A.	Retrospect	1.	A forward look or a view into the future for something
B.	Suspect	2.	A backward look or a view into the past
C.	Prospect	3.	To doubt the genuineness or truth of something
D.	Introspect	4.	A examination of one's motives or look looking inwards

Codes

	A	B	C	D		A	B	C	D
(a)	2	4	3	1	(b)	4	1	2	3
(c)	3	1	4	2	(d)	2	3	1	4

27. Consider the following statements.

1. The word that describes the compulsion to tell lies or in other words a habitual liar is known as Mythomania.
2. Someone who looks at the worst aspects of things is called an optimist.
3. The practice of marriage within one's own tribe is called as endogamy and the practice of marriage outside the tribe is exogamy.

Which of the these statements are correct?

(a) 1 and 2   (b) 2 and 3

(c) 1 and 3   (d) All of these

Reading Comprehension

Directions (Q. Nos. 1-5) Read the passage carefully and answer the questions that follow.

The sugar maple is a hard maple tree. It can grow as tall as 100 feet and as wide as 4 feet. The sugar maple is commercially valued for its sap, which is used in the making of maple syrup. Two states of the USA, Vermont and New York, rank as major producers of maple syrup. In Canada, the state of Quebec's annual syrup production is almost 1 million litres annually. To make pure maple syrup, holes are made in the trunk of the tree at the end of the winter or in early spring.

The water-like sap seeps through the holes and runs through a plastic spout that is put into the hole. Afterwards, the collected sap is transferred into tubes that are hooked up to a tank kept in the sugar house. Then the sap goes through the boiling process.

Boiling enhances the flavour as well as adding colour to the sap. Once the sugar content of the sap is about 65-66%, the sap is ready to be strained and marketed. The maple syrup found in the supermarkets, however, is usually not pure and has other additives.

The colour of pure maple may range from golden honey to light brown. Between 35 and 50 litres of sap is needed to produce 1 litre of maple syrup. Also popular for strength and finish of its wood, the sugar maple tree has been put to use in the making of furniture, interior woodwork, flooring and crates.

1. In the given passage, the author defines a ....
   (a) Sugar maple
   (b) A tank
   (c) Additives
   (d) Furniture

2. According to the passage, which of the following periods is ideal for sapping?
   (a) Early November to late December
   (b) February to early April
   (c) May to late July
   (d) August to early October

3. What can be inferred about the production of maple syrup?
   (a) The higher the volume, the less predictable the quality.
   (b) It is labour intensive.
   (c) Its processing demands complicated equipment.
   (d) It is rather simple, but time-consuming.

4. The word 'its' in the last sentence of the passage refers to
   (a) sap
   (b) maple syrup
   (c) colour
   (d) the sugar maple tree

5. Which state of the USA rank as the major producers of maple syrup?
   A. Vermont   B. New York
   C. Quebec
   (a) Only A   (b) Only B
   (c) Both A and B   (d) Both B and C

Directions (Q. Nos. 6-10) Read the comprehension based on a poem and answer the questions that follow.

Moonlight

Deep in the night
When all is still
A moon beam climbs the window-sill
Over your bed
It softly flies
To see if sleep has closed your eyes
A pinch of gold
Some fairy sand
It clasped within that moonbeam's hand
And if by chance
You're not asleep
It comes tip-toe on gentle feet
To touch your eyes
With golden beams
And take you to the land of dreams

6. The poet speaks of the moonlight as if it were a ....
   (a) watchman
   (b) thief
   (c) shadow
   (d) fairy

7. The poet has used the expressions 'A pinch of gold' and 'Some fairy sand' to describe the ....
   (a) Child's dream world
   (b) Colour of the moon
   (c) Face of an innocent child
   (d) Face of the moon

8. A soothing effect of the moonlight is ....
   (a) It puts child to sleep
   (b) It rubs a pinch of golden sand
   (c) It climbs the window-sill
   (d) It tip-toes on the gentle feet

9. The 'you' in the poem most probably is ....
   (a) The poet   (b) A mother
   (c) A little child   (d) A golden fairy

10. Which among the following lines describes the silent movement of the moon light?
    (a) Deep in the night
    (b) Everything is still
    (c) Comes tip-toe on gentle feet
    (d) Climbs the window-sill

Directions (Q. Nos. 11-15) Read the passage given below and answer the questions that follow.

Louis Braille was a Frenchman. He developed the famous touch method of the Braille system, by which millions of blind people read and write. Blind himself since the age of three, he realised that the existing methods for teaching the blind were not proper. So he worked for many years to find improved methods.

He also devised a stylus with which a blind person could easily make the dots. Braille employs a system of raised dots that represent letters, signs and numbers. A blind person reads Braille by touching the dots with his fingertips. The system can be adapted for use in any language.

The system may also be used for arithmetic and higher mathematics. The Braille system has also been used in games, such as chess, checkers and cards. Braille books are made of a thick, spongy paper on which the characters are embossed. The Braille symbols are large and thick, so that the fingers can feel their shape easily. They are set across the page like ordinary print, but because of their size, they require more space.

11. Why did Louis Braille work on improved methods for blind people?
    (a) Because existing methods of teaching were not proper.
    (b) Because he wanted to make learning easier for blind people.
    (c) Because methods required more research and time.
    (d) Both (a) and (b)

12. The system of Braille refers to ....
    (a) Dot method   (b) Touch method
    (c) Symbol method (d) Finger method

13. People who are blind can easily make the dots in the Braille system with the help of ....
    (a) letters   (b) symbols
    (c) signs   (d) stylus

14. Find the synonyms of the word 'Embossed'.
    (a) Disfigure   (b) Spoil
    (c) Deface   (d) Adorn

15. Find the incorrect statement about Braille system from the given options.
    (a) It can be used in any language.
    (b) Its symbols can be made on any type of sheet.

(c) It can also be used in Board and Cards game.
(d) It employs a system of raised dots which can be easily coded.

Directions (Q. Nos. 16-20) Read the comprehension based on a poem and answer the questions that follow.

Ring out, wild bells, to the wild sky,
The flying cloud, the frosty light:
The year is dying in the night;
Ring out, wild bells, and let him die.
Ring out the old, ring in the new,
Ring, happy bells, across the snow:
The year is going, let him go;
Ring out the false, ring in the true.
Ring out the grief that saps the mind,
For those that here we see no more;
Ring out the feud of rich and poor,
Ring in redress to all mankind.
Ring out a slowly dying cause,
And ancient forms of party strife;
Ring in the nobler modes of life,
With sweeter manners, purer laws.
–by Alfred, Lord Tennyson

16. What holiday would you associate with these lines?
    (a) Easter holidays
    (b) Summer holidays
    (c) Christmas and New Year holidays
    (d) None of the above

17. What kind of changes does Tennyson hope to see in the future?
    (a) Changes which cause wars and bitterness
    (b) Changes which cause people to become law-abiding
    (c) Changes which make the rich fight with the poor
    (d) Changes which cause happiness in all spheres of life

18. Which of the following does the poet not want to ring out?

(a) Good manners

(b) Quarrels between the poor and the rich

(c) Falsehood

(d) Sadness

19. What does 'redress' mean in this poem?

(a) Get dressed again / change clothes

(b) Clothing worn by an older person

(c) Making up for a wrong or injustice

(d) Playing melodious music

20. What is a feud, as given in the poem?

(a) An ongoing quarrel with bad feelings on each side

(b) A game that creates feelings of comfort

(c) A waterway that is similar to a deep river

(d) A home with separate living quarters for servants

Directions (Q. Nos. 21-25) Read the passage given below and answer the questions that follow.

Social networks are as old as the internet technology that was first developed in the 1960s. After 2003, the social networks became very popular. Currently, internet users have more than two hundred social networks to choose from. Techers, students and professionals can also create discussion, forums, or write blogs and posts to explore different and wide-ranging topics. On the other hand, many companies use social networks to connect with customers and clients. This can create opportunities for relationship-building, brand-building, publicity and promotions. However, there are several disadvantage of social networking sites as well. Cybercrime and cyber bullying have increased because it is hard to identify the offender and it is almost impossible to keep full-time surveillance in such a wide network.

As people spend more time on social networking sites, they experience less face-to-face interaction which also makes them more dependent on devices. Addiction to online networking is yet another disadvantage.

21. When did social networking sites witness more acceptances?

(a) 2000   (b) 2001

(c) 2003   (d) 2004

22. How does social networking impact learning?

(a) It helps people to share their ideas.

(b) Discussion forums help students to explore new information.

(c) It distracts students from studies.

(d) Both (a) and (b)

23. How do social networking sites increase crime?

(a) Due to increased number of users

(b) Due to addiction of social networking sites

(c) Due to easy accessibility

(d) All of the above

24. The word 'Offender' given in the passage is an antonyms of ....

(a) crook   (b) felon

(c) saviour   (d) fugitive

25. Social networking makes us dependent on ....

(a) devices

(b) internet

(c) face to face communication

(d) None of the above

Chapter 19

Writing Skills

1 Mark Questions

Directions (Q. Nos. 1-5) The parts of a formal letter are identified by numbers in the blank official letter format given below. Answer the questions 1 to 5 given below by selecting the correct option.

1. The item identified as '2' is
   (a) sender's address
   (b) subscription
   (c) salutation
   (d) date

2. The item identified as '1' is
   (a) receiver's name
   (b) receiver's address
   (c) body of letter
   (d) subject of the letter

3. The item identified as '3' is
   (a) sender's address
   (b) signature
   (c) salutation
   (d) date

4. The item identified as '7' is
   (a) sender's name
   (b) body of the letter
   (c) subject of letter
   (d) subscription

5. The item identified as '8' is
   (a) receiver's name/rank
   (b) receiver's address
   (c) salutation
   (d) subscription and signature

Directions (Q. Nos. 6-15) In the following letter, the linking words and phrases are missing. Choose the most appropriate word/ phrase to be filled in each blank from the options given.

25, Banjara Road
Hyderabad 500034

Dear Rakesh,

Remember that I told you I was trying to get a job at Dell Computers. Well, I finally managed to get one! Of course, I haven't been working there long, ...(6)....... I can already tell that it's a wonderful place to work in. All the staff and directors are very friendly and .....(7)....., they have marvellous facilities for employees. ......(8) ......, there's a bar and gym, and lots of other things. I'm called the Senior Safety Equipment Officer. May sound like an impressive title, but it's not a very ......(9) ...... of what I do. My main job is to provide protective clothing, ...(10)....... overalls, helmets and so on. I estimate what the different departments will need and then I order it from the ......(11)...... . ...(12) ...... I make sure that the various departments have everything they want. ......(13)...... I have to supply all the offices with paper, envelopes and so on. I find the job ......(14) ...... because I get the chance to go all over the factory and meet everyone. ......(15) ...... the pay is far better than in my old job. Anyway that's my news. What about yours? Drop me a line when you have time.

Regards to your parents and best wishes to you.

Abhijit Narang

6. (a) but   (b) because
    (c) and   (d) or

7. (a) what's more   (b) therefore
    (c) moreover   (d) so

8. (a) For instance   (b) However
    (c) Moreover   (d) Ever

9. (a) fine account
    (b) accurate description
    (c) correct picture
    (d) fine description

10. (a) namely   (b) as
    (c) such as   (d) like

11. (a) supply branch   (b) distribution
    (c) suppliers   (d) person

12. (a) By the way   (b) Any way
    (c) However   (d) In this way

13. (a) But   (b) Although
    (c) However   (d) Secondly

14. (a) very boring   (b) interesting
    (c) dull   (d) mind boggling

15. (a) Besides
    (b) On the other hand
    (c) In contrast
    (d) Beside

Directions (Q. Nos. 16-19) Fill in the blanks to complete the paragraph from an article.

It is believed that in near future the home appliances market would register a steady growth in which .....(16)...... would play a ......(17)...... role and would owe up to 65% of the revenue generated. Among the two categories of buyers the first ones are the people inclined towards buying only ....(18)...... items and second are people who demand more of .....(19)...... .

16. (a) marginal goods   (b) white goods
    (c) good   (d) unwanted goods

17. (a) pivotal   (b) insignificant   (c) hard   (d) no

18. (a) cheap   (b) bottom line   (c) sub-standard   (d) unbalanced

19. (a) expensive   (b) necessity   (c) good quality   (d) luxury goods

2 Marks Questions

Directions (Q. Nos. 20-25) A notice on the subject 'Blood Donation' has been issued by the Red Cross Blood Bank Society, which is given below with some parts missing, but numbered 20-25. The options for these missing words/phrases are given below the notice. Select the correct options to fill in the missing parts.

| 20 | , Delhi

20 May 20XX   **NOTICE**

| 21 |

A State Level function to observe a | 22 | is being organised on 28th and 29th May, 20XX at Red Cross | 23 |, Asif Ali Road, Delhi. The camp will begin at 8 AM and will continue till 5 PM on both days. | 24 | will be present to carry out the procedures. All are requested to take part in this | 25 |

Gaurav Sharma
President

---

20. (a) Salutation   (b) Name of governing body
    (c) Both (a) and (b)   (d) Name of event

21. (a) Name of event   (b) Name of governing body
    (c) Both (a) and (b)   (d) Salutation

22. (a) compulsory blood donation day   (b) voluntary blood donation day
    (c) partial blood donation day   (d) government blood donation day

23. (a) Blood bank office   (b) Society office
    (c) Blood bank hospital   (d) Blood donation camp

24. (a) A team of specialised doctors   (b) a team of doctors and assistants
    (c) a team of volunteer doctors   (d) a team of doctors and people

25. (a) great cause   (b) noble cause
    (c) greedy cause   (d) money-making cause

Communication Skills

1 Mark Questions

Directions (Q. Nos. 1-5) Select the correct option that defines the following sentences.

1. All the bank cheques should be written in legible writing and signed correctly.
   - (a) Fact
   - (b) Request
   - (c) Threat
   - (d) Opinion

2. If you are a non-native English speaker doing major in English then hats off to you.
   - (a) Opinion
   - (b) Order
   - (c) Fact
   - (d) Can't say

3. I was surprised to know that one liter of water weighs one kilogram.
   - (a) Threat
   - (b) Fact
   - (c) Opinion
   - (d) Can't say

4. Send me my account statement through email only and not by post.
   - (a) Opinion
   - (b) Fact
   - (c) Request
   - (d) Order

5. This building will soon blow up into tiny pieces and all of you will be killed.
   - (a) Order
   - (b) Threat
   - (c) Fact
   - (d) Request

Directions (Q. Nos. 6-10) Read the following statements and choose the correct option from the given alternatives.

6. Your married sister has not invited you to her birthday party, how will you react?
   - (a) Hold grudge against her
   - (b) Send her birthday wishes
   - (c) Attend the party somehow
   - (d) Ignore the whole situation

7. You are interviewed for a job. At that time, which of the following is most important for you?
   - (a) Looking for a reputed company
   - (b) Remuneration and other facilities
   - (c) Growth opportunities
   - (d) All of the above

8. While you board a train for a long journey, you notice an unclaimed bag lying underneath your seat, you would ....
   - (a) ignore it as it do not belongs to you
   - (b) open the bag to see if it contains something harmful
   - (c) report to the ticket checker
   - (d) finding no one to claim it, you take it

9. During the Geography examination, you found that you have not brought your pencil and cannot do the map work, what is the best thing you would do?
   - (a) Tell the examiner and ask if it can be arranged
   - (b) Not attempt the map questions
   - (c) Ask from students sitting around you
   - (d) Attempt questions without using pencil

10. You are living in a school hostel and you notice that there is lack of basic cleanliness in the toilets and rest rooms. What would be the best step?

  (a) Leave the hostel and return home

  (b) Complain to your parents about it

  (c) Bring the matter to the hostel in-charge

  (d) Ignore the matter altogether

Directions (Q. Nos. 11-18) Select the appropriate options to fill in the blanks in the telephonic conversation between Niti and Kartik.

Kartik: Hello, can I speak to Anirudh?

Niti: He is not at home right now. ....(11).......... ?

Kartik: This is Kartik, his friend...........(12)..........

Niti: .....(13)......, his sister.

Kartik: Hello Niti, ...(14)..........?

Niti: Anirudh ....(15).......... to attend his Maths coaching class.

Kartik: Ok, ...(16) ....

Niti: .....(17)..... .

Kartik: We have arranged a farewell party for our English instructor so ....(18)......

Niti: I will. Anything else?

Kartik: No, Thank you. Bye

Niti: Bye

11. (a) Who are you   (b) What is it

  (c) Who is speaking (d) What do you want

12. (a) May I know who is on the line?

  (b) would you tell me, who are you?

  (c) Could I know who is on the line?

  (d) Please care to tell me who is there?

13. (a) It is Niti   (b) She is Niti

  (c) This is Niti   (d) Aany of these

14. (a) what is Anirudh doing?

  (b) why Anirudh is not on the line

  (c) where is Anirudh?

  (d) where has Anirudh gone

15. (a) has gone out   (b) had gone out

  (c) have gone out   (d) was gone out

16. (a) give a message to Anirudh.

  (b) give him a message, will you?

  (c) can you please give him a message?

  (d) Note down the message and tell him.

17. (a) Ok, tell me   (b) Certainly

  (c) Sure, tell me   (d) Any of these

18. (a) therefore he might reach school early tomorrow.

  (b) ask him to reach school early tomorrow.

  (c) can he reach school early tomorrow?

  (d) in order to that he may reach school early tomorrow.

2 Marks Questions

19. The given conversation has mixed up sentences. Reorder them correctly.

  1. Hi, I will issue you a new cheque book.

  2. I make a lot of transactions so 50.

  3. Hello, my cheque book is finished.

  4. How many sheets do you want there to be?

  (a) 3-2-1-4   (b) 3-1-2-4

  (c) 3-1-4-2   (d) 3-4-2-1

20. Complete the conversation appropriately.

Father: What? You lost the car keys again?

Daughter: ....

Father: Don't you remember, I am sure, it isn't. You dropped it in the aquarium and we searched the whole house.

(a) Don't worry, I will find the car keys.
(b) Your car was not in good condition either.
(c) What do you mean again?
(d) Not again, it is for the first time.

21. Situation-Reaction test.

    During an overnight bus journey, at mid night you suddenly wake up by a certain sound. When you looked around, you found that someone is trying to steal a bag from the overhead rack. You would

    (a) hit him with something sharp.
    (b) raise alarm and call the conductor.
    (c) Dial 100 from your mobile.
    (d) ignore and pretend to sleep.

22. Fill in the blanks to complete the conversation given below.

    Receptionist: Sir, if you want a hotel room with the view of the mountain side or the valley side, then it will be ....
    Client: Ok, what is the difference in the .... then?
    Receptionist: I'll just .... and tell you.

    (a) cheaper, rent, ask
    (b) costly, room, see
    (c) cheap, between, find
    (d) costlier, fare, check

23. In this question two statements are given. Find out which of these sentence is a fact and which is an opinion. Mark F for Fact and O for Opinion.

    1. Rampant air pollution is a very likely cause of the ongoing epidemic.
    2. American business generates enough paper to circle the earth 20 times.

    (a) 1-F, 2-O   (b) 1-O, 2-F
    (c) 1-F, 2-F   (d) 1-O, 2-O

24. In this question three statements are given. Find out which of these sentence is a fact /opinion/request. Mark F for Fact, O for Opinion and R for Request.

    1. Keep smiling, even if you feel terribly disgusted.
    2. Natural world encompasses all living and nonliving things occurring naturally.
    3. If this continues then the earth will soon turn into a desert or be covered in sea water.

    (a) 1-F, 2-R, 3-O
    (b) 1-O, 2-R, 3-F
    (c) 1-O, 2-F, 3-R
    (d) 1-R, 2-F, 3-O

25. Match the following to form complete sentences.

	List-I		List-II
A.	Recycling one aluminum can save energy	1.	Upto 30 per cent of the cold air escapes.
B.	Every time you open the refrigerator door	2.	Made up of packaging materials.
C.	About one-third of an average landfill is	3.	Into the ocean kills many sea creatures.
D.	Plastic bags and plastic garbage thrown	4.	To run a TV for three hours.

Codes

	A	B	C	D
(a)	1	4	3	2
(b)	4	1	2	3
(c)	3	1	4	2
(d)	2	3	1	4

PRACTICE SET 01

1 Mark Questions

Directions (Q. Nos. 1-5) Read the passage carefully and select the option that you consider the most appropriate answer to each question.

The Story of Aspirin

Before people started using aspirin as a drug to relieve pain, there was willow bark. Around 400 BC, Hippocrates, the 'father of medicine', advised chewing it to ease the pain of childbirth. For centuries, people all over the world knew of its power to treat headache, fever and inflammation. However, they did not understand why it had this power.

Through the 19th century, Chemistry became an important development in science. In Germany in the 1820s, the magic chemical in willow bark was isolated and named *salicin*. Later in the century, a drug, *acetylsalicyclic acid*, was developed, but no one really knew what to do with it. Some people tried a crude form of the drug which, they said, burned in their stomachs like acid.

Then a young chemist at the German chemical firm of Bayer & Company decided to try *acetylsalicyclic acid* on his father, who had arthritis. The wonder drug, aspirin, was born!

Why it was named *aspirin* is still debated. One theory is that the word came from *spiraea*, the plant from which *salicin* was actually isolated. The first aspirin tablets that people could buy from chemists' shops appeared at the beginning of the 20th century.

1. What does the first sentence of the passage tell us?
   (a) People have always known about both willow bark and aspirin as pain relievers.
   (b) People used willow bark to ease pain before aspirin was developed.
   (c) Long ago, people knew how to use aspirin to relieve pain.
   (d) Since ancient days people knew how to extract aspirin from willow bark.

2. In the second sentence of the passage, the word 'it' refers to ....
   (a) a drug   (b) medicine
   (c) aspirin   (d) willow bark

3. According to the passage, Hippocrates knew ....
   (a) why willow bark could ease pain
   (b) how willow bark could be processed
   (c) what willow bark could be used for
   (d) All of the above

4. The word 'wonder' used in the third paragraph is nearest in meaning to ....
   (a) marvellous   (b) admiration
   (c) surprise   (d) sensation

5. According to the passage, "The wonder drug, aspirin, was born!" when a young German chemist ....
   (a) was able to produce acetylsalicyclic acid
   (b) was able to prevent his father's arthritis
   (c) used acetylsalicyclic acid to reduce his father's pain
   (d) produced a drug combining salicin and acetylsalicyclic acid

6. In the passage below, the first and last sentences are identified as A and Z. The remaining four sentences are labelled as P, Q, R and S. Find the correct sequence of these four sentences and select the correct option accordingly.

A The Hound of the Baskervilles was feared by people of the area.

P The animal's shadowy silhouette did not reveal any details about it.

Q Nobody had in reality seen the hound.

R Some people spoke of seeing a huge, shadowy form of a hound at midnight on the moor.

S And they spoke of it in tones of grave horror.

Z Thus, the hound remained a perplexing mystery.

(a) PQRS   (b) QPSR

(c) RPQS   (d) RSQP

7. Find the option which is different from the others in any respect. This means that one of the four given options does not belong to the group of the other three.

(a) Duckling   (b) Chicks

(c) Goat   (d) Calf

Directions (Q. Nos. 8 and 9) Select the option having the meaning nearest to the idioms underlined in the given sentences.

8. The celebratory party got <u>out of hand</u>, so we had to abruptly end it.

(a) out of control   (b) short of food

(c) short of hands   (d) restrained

9. Karan was <u>in hot water</u>, as he forgot to finish his homework.

(a) clean

(b) bathed properly

(c) happy

(d) in trouble

10. Change the sentence given below into reported speech and accordingly select the best option.

"I slipped and fell down the stairs yesterday", said Sharmila.

(a) Sharmila remarked that she had slipped and fallen down the stairs yesterday.

(b) Sharmila said that she has slipped and fallen down the stairs yesterday.

(c) Sharmila said that she had slipped and fallen down the stairs the previous day.

(d) Sharmila was saying that she slipped and fell down the stairs the previous day.

11. Change the sentence given below into a simple sentence and accordingly select the best option.

It was raining heavily, so many trains were cancelled.

(a) It was raining heavily due to which many trains were cancelled.

(b) On account of heavy rains, many trains were cancelled.

(c) Accounting for the heavy rains, many trains were cancelled.

(d) Many trains were cancelled due to the heavy rain.

12. Change the sentence given below to passive voice using the underlined word as subject and accordingly select the best option.

They still deny <u>women</u> the right to vote in Switzerland.

(a) Switzerland does not allow women to have voting rights.

(b) Switzerland does not allow women to have the right to vote.

(c) Women in Switzerland can't vote.

(d) Women are still denied the right to vote in Switzerland.

Directions (Q. Nos. 13 and 14) Find the synonyms for the words underlined in the sentences below and accordingly select the best option.

13. The <u>benevolent</u> industrialist offered many scholarships for bright school students to study medicine.
   (a) generous   (b) industrious
   (c) helpless   (d) unkind

14. The homes of the Bedouins are <u>portable</u> because the tribe is nomadic.
   (a) temporary   (b) tough
   (c) transportable   (d) convenient

Directions (Q. Nos. 15 and 16) Identify the grammatically incorrect sentence from the given options.

15. (a) The constructed new bridge took three years.
   (b) Animals make the most complicated homes.
   (c) The result of the first experiment was satisfactory.
   (d) Eradication of poverty is the need of the hour.

16. (a) His rudeness reinforced my determination to leave him.
   (b) She was in complete bewilderment when her husband suddenly left her.
   (c) This drug has absolutely no chemical similarity to any other drug.
   (d) Names of players who will be included in team have been announced.

Directions (Q. Nos. 17 and 18) Fill in the blanks with the correct form of verb.

17. You .... to be punctual.
   (a) should   (b) ought
   (c) would   (d) must

18. He .... play cricket in his youth.
   (a) used to   (b) was used to
   (c) is used to   (d) were used to

Directions (Q. Nos. 19 and 20) Fill in the blanks with the most appropriate article.

19. Hearing the speech of their leader, the crowd was in .... state of Euphoria.
   (a) a   (b) an
   (c) the   (d) no article required

20. "Please lay .... extra plate for dinner", Malti told her cook.
   (a) a   (b) an
   (c) the   (d) no article required

Directions (Q. Nos. 21 and 22) Fill in the blanks with the most appropriate preposition.

21. I don't always agree .... what my parents tell me.
   (a) at   (b) with
   (c) to   (d) after

22. It is not good, running away .... your loved ones.
   (a) with   (b) to
   (c) from   (d) of

23. Punctuate the given sentence to make it meaningful and accordingly select the best option.

You must bring the following to the examination a pen a ruler a pencil an eraser and your hall ticket

   (a) You must bring the following to the examination; a pen, a ruler, a pencil, an eraser, and your hall ticket?
   (b) You must bring the following to the examination, a pen, a ruler, a pencil, an eraser, and your hall ticket.
   (c) You must bring the following to the examination; a pen, a ruler, a pencil, an eraser, and your hall ticket.
   (d) You must bring the following to the examination: a pen, a ruler, a pencil, an eraser and your hall ticket.

Directions (Q. Nos. 24 and 25) Fill in the blanks with the most appropriate conjunction.

24. She practiced well .... she could win the match.
(a) such that   (b) so that
(c) and   (d) as well as

25. .... I had seen the red light, I would have stopped.
(a) If   (b) When (c) As (d) Though

Directions (Q. Nos. 26 and 27) A notice is given below with some parts missing, but substituted by rectangles with numbers 26 and 27. Identify the text which the numbers may be substituted by from the options given below.

XYZ Public School, Delhi
NOTICE

27

16th November, 2012

All the Activity Council members are informed to attend a meeting tomorrow at 10:30 AM in the Biology lab. The meeting is called to discuss the activites for Christmas Day. You should come with your ideas and the estimated cost as well as the infrastructure required. For further details please contact the undersigned.

26

Class X
(Activity Coordinator)

26. (a) Yours sincerely
(b) St Mary's Higher Secondary School
(c) Class Monitor
(d) Arvind Solanki

27. (a) Christmas Day Celebrations
(b) St Xavier's High School
(c) Important Meeting
(d) Yours sincerely

Directions (Q. Nos. 28-30) Fill in the blank with the correct tense of the verb given in bracket immediately after the blank.

28. My mother .... (stay) in a rented house for three years.
(a) has stayed
(b) had staying
(c) has been staying
(d) staying

29. Irfan .... (undergo) treatment for the past one year for his tumor.
(a) has been undergoing
(b) is been undergoing
(c) has already undergone
(d) has underwent

30. The doctor who treats Satya .... (say) that he .... (discharge) tomorrow from the nursing home.
(a) said, will be discharge
(b) has said, would be discharged
(c) says, would be discharged
(d) says, will be discharged

Directions (Q. Nos. 31 and 32) State if the sentence is an order/request/fact /opinion.

31. Childhood is the period of life where the seeds of character are sown.
(a) Fact   (b) Opinion
(c) Request   (d) Order

32. Passengers are warned not to lean out of the window when the train is in motion.
(a) Fact   (b) Opinion
(c) Request   (d) Order

Directions (Q. Nos. 33 and 34) Identify the pronouns in the given sentence.

33. Beena failed miserably in her exam and now she has vowed not to give any other examination.
(a) Beena, she, miserably, has, other
(b) She, her, any

(c) Examination, vowed, now

(d) Her, exam, she

34. Ulysses asked the little bird whether it had anything to tell him.

(a) It, anything, him

(b) Ulysses, little, it, had

(c) The, it, had, him, anything

(d) It, him

35. In the question below, the first and last sentences of the paragraph are given put the rest of the sentences in correct order.

The tribal settlement is called Podu.

P. The huts have entrances as low as three to four feet.

Q. It is located in a safe place, sheltered from wild animals.

R. Bamboo is used along with sticks and twigs to make the walls, which are then plastered with mud to a height of about three feet.

S. It usually consists of a group of ten to fifty huts.

The roof is made of bamboo mesh, dried grass and tree bark.

(a) PQRS

(b) QPSR

(c) SPQR

(d) QSPR

36. Find the option that is different from the others.

(a) Cock

(b) Drake

(c) Doe

(d) Bull

Directions (Q. Nos. 37-39) Identify the grammatically correct sentence from the given sentences.

37. (a) Harleen met Mohit on the first last of this month.

(b) Although the money was missing, Sarita has not taken it.

(c) Lata is good at playing instruments and the guitar.

(d) Please don't use your nail as a screwdriver.

38. (a) You may cultivate your hobbies as long as they do not interfere with your studies.

(b) Kailash has being informed of the gravity in the situation.

(c) I was indignant at the way Ashok was treated his servants.

(d) Vishal has been hostile against me right since the beginning.

39. (a) As the weather was rough, the sailors cancelled the voyage across the channel.

(b) The sailor cancel the voyage across the channel because the whether was rough.

(c) The weather had being rough, the sailors cancelled the voyage.

(d) The weather was so rough and so the sailor have to cancel their voyage.

40. Select the option nearest in meaning to the underlined words.

Damayanti crossed her fingers, wishing it would not rain on her wedding day.

(a) prayed

(b) hoped for good luck

(c) became cheerful

(d) day dreamed

2 Marks Questions

41. Consider the following statements.

1. They got married after they had to learn to manage their own home.
2. Sandeep went crazy due to his wife Meena burnt his breakfast.

Which of these sentences uses the connectors after and due correctly?

(a) Only 1   (b) Only 2
(c) Both 1 and 2   (d) None of these

42. Fill in the blanks with correct words to make a meaningful passage.

Today, my mom and I .... a cake for my dad's birthday. We .... the flour into a bowl. We crack eggs and add them to the bowl. Next, mom .... in milk and sugar. We put the batter in a mould and place it into the oven and wait.

(a) will bake, take, mixes
(b) bake, takes, mix
(c) bake, take, mix
(d) will bake, takes, mix

43. Read the stanza taken from a poem and answer the following question.
Did I ever stop to make you laugh
When your light stopped shining for a while?
When your world seemed almost torn in half,
When you'd lost your way or missed a choice,
Did I let you know that I was near.
Which word in the poem means ripped apart?

(a) Stopped   (b) Torn
(c) Lost   (d) Know

44. Replace the underlined words with the correct words to make a meaningful paragraph.

The stress of work, the frustration of the <u>easy going</u> life and the irritation of being constantly on the move is often <u>mistaken</u> when a person is driving. This is precisely the <u>temper</u> why many people often end up fighting with other people driving, riding or walking on the road.

(a) Dull and boring, managed, anger
(b) Hectic, expressed, reason
(c) Tough, happened, result
(d) Routine, associated, rage

45. Match the following to form complete sentences.

	List-I		List-II
A.	Kishore has green fingers because	1.	Was robbing when the police entered.
B.	The thief was caught red handed as he	2.	Tried to steal from the cookie jar.
C.	His mother was very angry when he	3.	You should be fine, so don't worry.
D.	If you carry on as you've been doing,	4.	Everything grows so well in his garden.

Codes

	A	B	C	D		A	B	C	D
(a)	1	4	3	2	(b)	4	1	2	3
(c)	3	1	4	2	(d)	2	3	1	4

46. Choose from the options the part of the sentence that has an error.

Mary doesn't like cartoons because they is loud, so she doesn't watch them.

(a) Mary doesn't like
(b) Cartoons because they
(c) is loud, so she
(d) doesn't watch them

47. Consider the following statements.

1. I'm half French: my mother is English but my father was born in Paris.

2. Romeo and Juliet was written by the greatest playwrights William Shakespeare.

3. Mount Everest is not actually the most highest mountain on Earth, there are so many under the ocean.

Which of the these statements are grammatically incorrect ?

(a) 1 and 2 (b) 2 and 3

(c) 1 and 3 (d) None of these

48. Consider the following statements.

1. 'Approve', 'praise' and 'compliment' are antonyms of condemn.

2. 'Insignificant', 'trivial' and 'consequential' are antonyms of momentous.

Which of these statement is/are correct?

(a) Only 1

(b) Only 2

(c) Both 1 and 2

(d) None of the above

49. Match the following one words with their meanings.

List-I		List-II
A. Telegraph	1.	The school or college one attends
B. Podium	2.	A place for feet or a speaker's platform

List-I		List-II
C. Alma Mater	3.	Make to happen at the same time
D. Synchronise	4.	A written message from a far off place

Codes

	A	B	C	D		A	B	C	D
(a)	4	2	1	3	(b)	4	1	2	3
(c)	3	4	2	1	(d)	2	4	3	1

50. Match the following.

List-I	List-II	List-III
A. Sonia had no idea she	1. Time to celebrate; so we're going	I. Was a few years ago.
B. Our exams are over and it's	2. He told her he'd sold their	II. The news came out of the blue.
C. We go to restaurants once	3. Was going to lose her job	III. Cow for a sackful of grain.
D. Guru's mother saw red when	4. In a blue moon, as the last time	IV. To paint the town red.

Codes

(a) A-4-I, B-3-IV, C-2-II, D-1-III

(b) A-4-I, B-1-IV, C-2-III, D-3-II

(c) A-3-II, B-1-IV, C-4-I, D-2-III

(d) A-2-II, B-1-III, C-4-II, D-3-III

PRACTICE SET 02

Directions (Q. Nos. 1-5) Read the passage carefully and select the option that you consider the most appropriate answer to each question.

The History of Ice-Cream

George Washington went into debt over it, Nero sent slaves across his empire due to it and the success of modern day cafès owes a huge debt to it.

It is, of course, ice-cream. The Chinese are credited with being the first to add salt and saltpetre to snow or pounded ice to lower its freezing temperature in order to make frozen dairy dishes. Some experts claim that the process may have started during the Han Dynasty (206 BC - 220 AD), but food writers Weir and Liddell only present evidence from the Tang period (618 AD - 907 AD). However, the love of iced desserts and drinks dates back much further; the earliest ice-house (2250 BC) was unearthed in Iraq.

Nero loved his 'slushees' of snow flavoured with honey, fruit and wine. The Arab world had their 'charabs' and the Turks their 'chorbets'. Even Alexander the Great, after his conquest of Egypt in 332 BC, had 15 trenches dug and filled with snow for his cooled 'punches'!

The 1660s saw water ices in Spain and Italy as well as in the cities of Vienna and Paris, while Venice had its iced creams. However, it took the birth of the cafe to make them a popular fashion. When a Sicilian named Procope opened Paris' first cafe in 1686, it was the sorbets and ice-creams that entranced Parisian society as much as the coffee. Within 100 years, iced desserts had captivated diners from the USA to London to Scandinavia.

In the 1850s, an editor of The Age newspaper in Melbourne, James Harrison, invented the ice-maker and the refrigerator, thus making ice more readily available throughout the year.

1. The main purpose of the text is to ....
   (a) compare differences in iced desserts between cultures
   (b) document the process of making iced desserts
   (c) recount the development of iced desserts
   (d) explain the popularity of iced desserts

2. In the third paragraph, the writer uses quotation marks around the words 'slushees' and 'punches' to show that ....
   (a) he wants to emphasise them
   (b) he is using sarcasm
   (c) they are modern terms
   (d) they are taken from another text

3. According to the passage, the earliest discovered evidence for the consumption of iced desserts and drinks dates back to ....
   (a) 2250 BC
   (b) 322 BC
   (c) 206 BC - 220 AD
   (d) 618 AD - 907 AD

4. Due to James Harrison's inventions
....
   (a) iced desserts became readily available in London
   (b) iced desserts could be made throughout the year
   (c) a wider range of ice-cream flavours could be created
   (d) paper cups or dishes were not needed to serve ice-cream

5. In the fourth paragraph the word 'captivated' is nearest in meaning to
....
   (a) apprehended
   (b) enthralled
   (c) captured
   (d) arrested

6. Find the antonym of the word underlined in the sentence below and accordingly select the best option.

   Sunil <u>admitted</u> his mistake in cheating during the final exams.
   (a) abandoned   (b) repulsed
   (c) challenged   (d) denied

7. Change the sentence given below into direct speech and accordingly select the best option.

   My friend asked me when I usually got up.
   (a) My friend asked me, "When you usually got up?"
   (b) My friend said to me, "When do you usually got up?"
   (c) My friend said to me, "When do you usually get up?"
   (d) My friend questioned me, "When do you get up, usually?"

8. Change the sentence given below to active voice and accordingly select the best option.
   The instructions were being read out by the supervisor.
   (a) The supervisor is reading out the instructions.
   (b) The supervisor was reading out the instructions.
   (c) The supervisor had been reading out the instructions.
   (d) The supervisor will reading out the instructions.

Directions (Q. Nos. 9 and 10) Fill in the blanks using appropriate tense forms and accordingly select the best option.

9. We .... the old man to the hospital last evening.
   (a) took
   (b) take
   (c) have taken
   (d) had taken

10. More and more people .... their headphones to .... to music.
   (a) used, listening
   (b) are used, listened
   (c) using, listened
   (d) are using, listen

Directions (Q. Nos. 11-13) Fill in the blanks using appropriate articles or determiners and accordingly select the best option.

11. We met .... nice European girls on holiday.
   (a) an   (b) the
   (c) some   (d) any

12. I prefer .... mountains to the seaside.
   (a) a
   (b) the
   (c) some
   (d) many

13. .... umbrella is of no use in .... thunderstorm.
   (a) An, a
   (b) The, an
   (c) Many, a
   (d) An, the

14. Choose the option that is a synonym of the underlined word in the sentence given below.

The town-house is also a <u>noteworthy</u> building and contains large and important archives.
   (a) Inconspicuous
   (b) Ordinary
   (c) Significant
   (d) Standard

Directions (Q. Nos. 15 and 16) Select the option having the meaning nearest to the idioms underlined in the given sentences.

15. Why don't you make a simple website for your business? <u>There's nothing to it.</u>
   (a) It's like eating cake
   (b) It doesn't require any money
   (c) It's very easy
   (d) It's not impossible

16. At the start of the meeting, Saurabh tried to <u>break the ice</u> by cracking a joke.
   (a) cool frayed tempers
   (b) sway opinion
   (c) entertain the opposite side
   (d) initiate interaction

Directions (Q. Nos. 17 and 18) Identify the grammatically incorrect sentence from the given options.

17. (a) Last year I visited Australia for the first time.
   (b) The Mathematics teacher punished the boy because he hadn't made his homework.
   (c) Ramesh was in a hurry, so he couldn't talk to me.
   (d) Devinder fell off the ladder and fractured his leg.

18. (a) I went to Mussoorie for a holiday.
   (b) I have cleaned the entire house except for the bathroom.
   (c) Take the second turning on the left to reach the bus stand.
   (d) The Delhi Vidhan Sabha consisting of seventy members.

Directions (Q. Nos. 19 and 20) Punctuate the given sentence to make it meaningful and accordingly select the best option.

19. do you know if shes eligible and if she is eligible can she start the job tomorrow
   (a) Do you know if she's eligible, and if she is eligible can she start the job tomorrow?
   (b) Do you know if she's eligible and, if she is eligible, can she start the job tomorrow?
   (c) Do you know if she's eligible, and if she is eligible can she start the job tomorrow.
   (d) Do you know if she's eligible and if she is eligible, can she start the job tomorrow?

20. i am going Rizwan said to ask you a difficult question but you don't have to answer it
   (a) "I am going," Rizwan said, "to ask you a difficult question, but don't you have to answer it?"

(b) "I am" going, Rizwan said, "to ask you a difficult question, but don't you have to answer it?"

(c) "I am going," Rizwan said, "to ask you a difficult question but you don't have to answer it?"

(d) "I am going," Rizwan said, "to ask you a difficult question, but you don't have to answer it."

Directions (Q. Nos. 21 and 22) A formal letter is given below with some parts missing, but substituted by rectangles with numbers 21 and 22. Identify the text which the numbers may be substituted by from the options given below.

Customer Service Department
Saurabh Educational Publishers

| 21 |

11th April 20XX

Mr Girish Khurana
741, MG Road, Hapur - 245101

Subject: Books Received in Damaged Condition

Dear Mr Khurana

Thank you for your letter dated 7th April 20XX regarding books sent by us through courier being received in damaged condition by you. We have contacted the courier agency responsible regarding this problem and will get back to you shortly. We cannot accept any blame in the matter, as we had packed the books securely.

We regret the inconvenience caused.

| 22 |

Despatch Officer

---

21. (a) A well-known publisher
    (b) 45 Sarvodaya Nagar, Meerut -250001
    (c) First floor, Convenience Mall
    (d) c/o Educational Courier Service

22. (a) With love
    (b) Hope to see you soon
    (c) Yours sincerely
    (d) Saurabh Educational Publishers

23. Find the option which is different from the others in any respect. This means that one of the four given options does not belong to the group of the other three.
    (a) Cub   (b) Bitch
    (c) Dog   (d) Puppy

24. Fill in the blank with the most appropriate conjunction and accordingly select the best option.

    Other planets have small moons .... ours is very large compared to others.
    (a) and   (b) that
    (c) but   (d) as well as

Directions (Q. Nos. 25 and 26) Fill in the blank with the most appropriate preposition and accordingly select the best option.

25. Rupesh had really no excuse .... attacking that press photographer.
    (a) in   (b) of
    (c) from   (d) for

26. The young Major Jarnail Singh was entrusted .... the task of suppressing the riots.
    (a) for   (b) with
    (c) to   (d) onto

Directions (Q. Nos. 27-30) Fill in the blanks with the correct verb form.

27. You .... for me. I could have reached there on my own.

(a) couldn't wait
(b) didn't need to wait
(c) needn't have waited
(d) need not wait

28. I don't think that I .... be able to come.

(a) could   (b) would
(c) can   (d) can't

29. I was worried that if I asked him again, he .... refuse.

(a) Should   (b) can
(c) may   (d) might

30. If you .... see him, give him my regards.

(a) Will
(b) would
(c) should
(d) shall

Directions (Q. Nos. 31 and 32) Fill in the blanks appropriately.

31. Talib Hussain said that .... safest place in India was .... sleeper class compartment in .... express train.

(a) a, an, the
(b) the, the, an
(c) the, some, any
(d) any, the, an

32. It is .... responsibility of .... government to protect .... private property.

(a) the, the , No word needed
(b) the, any, some
(c) No word needed, the, any
(d) a, the, any

33. Punctuate the following sentence to make it meaningful and accordingly select the best option.

When the teacher commented that her spelling was poor karuna replied all the members of my family are poor spellers why not me

(a) When the teacher commented that her spelling was poor, Karuna replied, "All the members of my family are poor spellers. Why not me?"

(b) When the teacher commented that her spelling was poor Karuna replied, all the members of my family are poor spellers, why not me?

(c) When the teacher commented that her spelling was poor karuna replied, "all the members of my family are poor spellers why not me?"

(d) When the teacher commented that her Spelling was poor, Karuna replied, all the members of my family are poor spellers, why not me?

Directions (Q. Nos. 34-36) An email is given below with some parts missing. Identify the text which may be substituted in the missing parts-

To: Sara124@gmail.com
CC:...............(34)...............
...............(35)............... Important email
Dear Sir,
Action is being taken on your complaint. Kindly bear with us till the next mail message you receive from us.
With regards
...............(36)...............

34. (a) Sarvesh Ahuja
(b) Marketing manager
(c) Kailash234@gmail.com
(d) Pravesh*4321

35. (a) BCC
(b) Subject
(c) Topic
(d) Salutation

36. (a) see you again
(b) thanking you
(c) Saurabh Educational Publishers
(d) Sarvesh Ahuja, Service Department

Directions (Q. Nos. 37 and 38) Find the statement that is grammatically correct.

37. (a) The history teacher punished the students who had not done their homework.
(b) The students who do not do their homework was being punished by the History teacher.
(c) The teacher who teaches us History punished those students who have not done their homework.
(d) The students who had not their homework were punished by our teacher which teaches History.

38. (a) All the milk have been drunk by our pet cat Tumi.
(b) Our pet cat named Tumi has drunk all the milk.
(c) The cat called Tumi has been drunk all the milk.
(d) All the milk is drink by our pet cat Tumi.

39. Choose the option that correctly changes the given sentence into direct speech.

Ravinder asked me if I could solve that problem.
(a) I asked Ravinder, "Can you solve this problem?"
(b) "Can you solve this problem?", Ravinder asked me.
(c) I asked Ravinder, "Could you solve this problem?"
(d) "Could you solve this problem?", Ravinder asked me.

40. Consider the following statements.
1. I won't invite my classmates to a party until I know them well.
2. He fell asleep while I was watching the thrilling movie.

Which of these sentences use the connectors until and while correctly?
(a) Only 1　　(b) Only 2
(c) Both 1 and 2　　(d) None of these

41. State True or False where T stands for grammatically correct statement and F stands for incorrect statements.
1. By the time my husband arrived home, I had already cleaned the house.
2. The first question paper was easy where this one are extremely difficult and tricky.
(a) 1-T, 2-F　　(b) 1-F, 2-T
(c) 1-T, 2-T　　(d) 1-F, 2-F

42. Read the stanza taken from a poem and answer the following question.

Ring out the old, ring in the new,
Ring out the grief that saps the mind,
For those that here we see no more,
Ring out the feud of rich and poor,
Ring in redress to all mankind.

What does the word 'Redress' mean in this poem?
(a) Get dressed again/ change clothes
(b) Clothing worn by an older person
(c) Making up for a wrong or an injustice
(d) Playing melodious music

43. Match the following to form complete sentences.

	List-I		List-II
A.	We spent more last month than we	1.	earned, so we are in the red again.
B.	Those campers are really green, they	2.	photocopier had broken down.

List-I	List-II
C. The baby screamed loudly when his	3. little sister took his toys away.
D. I tried to have more run down but the	4. have no idea how to set up a tent.

Codes

	A	B	C	D			A	B	C	D
(a)	1	4	3	2	(b)	4	1	2	3
(c)	3	1	4	2	(d)	2	3	1	4

44. Replace the underlined words with the correct words to make a meaningful paragraph.

A system, in order to run smoothly, needs fuel in the form of taxes and this fuel is <u>intercepted</u> in the economy of a country. Governments have big <u>finances</u> and the tax money plays a vital role in <u>terminating</u> many tasks perceived by the government.

(a) Generated, financial planning, completing

(b) Submitted, planning, rejecting

(c) Injected, budgets, accomplishing

(d) Computed, structures, assimilating

45. Arrange the following sentences in proper order.

1. The economy of Singapore is competitive and the

2. System is relatively free from corruption. According to reports,

3. Singapore ranks 15 and 14 in imports and exports, respectively.

4. extremely advanced country with a flourishing

5. is considered as one of the most business friendly nation.

6. In the present time, Singapore is considered to be an

7. Economy. It is considered as one of the Four Asian Tigers and

(a) 2751634

(b) 6475123

(c) 7416253

(d) 5173652

46. Consider the following statements.

1. My eyes are not as good as they were. I think I need glasses.

2. The Olympic Games are consecutive held after a period of every four years.

3. "Please slow down, because you're driving too fast!" said the annoyed girl.

Which of the these statements are grammatically correct?

(a) 1 and 2

(b) 2 and 3

(c) 1 and 3

(d) None of the above

47. In the passage below, the first and last sentences are identified as A and Z. The remaining four sentences are labelled as P, Q, R and S. Find the correct sequence of these four sentences and select the correct option accordingly.

A Abraham Lincoln managed a shop for a few months during his youth.

P Lincoln would jump up, attend to the customer's needs and then go back to his reading.

Q Sometimes a chance customer would come to his shop.

R He used to lie full length on the counter of the shop reading a book.

S Abraham's method of running the shop was totally different from others.

Z Never before or after had young Abraham got so much time for reading as he had in those days.

(a) PQRS

(b) RPSQ

(c) SRQP

(d) RSQP

48. Consider the following statements.

1. 'Late', 'tonight', 'recently' and 'still' are adverbs of time.
2. 'Here', 'upstairs', 'outside' and 'upwards' are adverbs of place.
3. 'Hardly', 'almost', 'rarely' and 'generally' are adverbs of frequency.

Which of these statements are correct?

(a) 1 and 2
(b) 2 and 3
(c) 1 and 3
(d) All of the above

49. Match the following.

	List-I		List-II		List-III
A.	If he'd used his grey cells,	1	Going to lose the job,	I	Some recreational activities.
B.	Jatin had no idea he was	2	Got enough money to	II	A stupid thing to do.
C.	Our exams are over and	3	He'd have realised it was	III	Pay the grocery bill.
D.	I am afraid I haven't	4	Its time to relax and do	IV	It came out of the blue.

Codes

(a) A-4-I, B-3-IV, C-2-II, D-1-III
(b) A-4-I, B-1-IV, C-2-III, D-3-II
(c) A-3-II, B-1-IV, C-4-I, D-2-III
(d) A-2-II, B-1-III, C-4-II, D-3-III

50. Choose from the options the part of the sentence that has an error.

We were lost in the woods, but my brother has a maps in his backpack.

(a) We were lost in the woods,
(b) but my brother
(c) has a maps
(d) in his backpack

ANSWERS

Chapter 1   Nouns

1. (b)	**2.** (b)	**3.** (a)	**4.** (d)	**5.** (c)	**6.** (b)	**7.** (a)	**8.** (b)	**9.** (a)	**10.** (a)
11. (b)	**12.** (a)	**13.** (a)	**14.** (d)	**15.** (c)	**16.** (a)	**17.** (b)	**18.** (b)	**19.** (c)	**20.** (a)
21. (d)	**22.** (b)	**23.** (c)	**24.** (b)	**25.** (c)	**26.** (c)	**27.** (c)	**28.** (i) (a), (ii) (c)		
29. (i)(b), (ii) (a)	**30.** (d)	**31.** (b)							

Chapter 2   Pronouns

1. (c)	**2.** (c)	**3.** (a)	**4.** (c)	**5.** (b)	**6.** (a)	**7.** (c)	**8.** (b)	**9.** (c)	**10.** (d)
11. (b)	**12.** (a)	**13.** (b)	**14.** (a)	**15.** (c)	**16.** (c)	**17.** (a)	**18.** (a)	**19.** (c)	**20.** (d)
21. (b)	**22.** (a)	**23.** (c)	**24.** (d)	**25.** (b)	**26.** (i) (c), (ii) (a)	**27.** (i) (c), (ii) (b)			

Chapter 3   Verbs

1. (c)	**2.** (d)	**3.** (a)	**4.** (c)	**5.** (d)	**6.** (b)	**7.** (c)	**8.** (b)	**9.** (c)	**10.** (b)
11. (a)	**12.** (c)	**13.** (a)	**14.** (d)	**15.** (b)	**16.** (a)	**17.** (b)	**18.** (c)	**19.** (i)(c), (ii)(a)	**20.** (c)
21. (d)	**22.** (d)	**23.** (b)	**24.** (i) (a), (ii) (c)						

Chapter 4   Adverbs

1. (c)	**2.** (a)	**3.** (c)	**4.** (b)	**5.** (a)	**6.** (c)	**7.** (b)	**8.** (a)	**9.** (b)	**10.** (c)
11. (c)	**12.** (a)	**13.** (a)	**14.** (d)	**15.** (a)	**16.** (d)	**17.** (b)	**18.** (a)	**19.** (i)(b), (ii)(a)	**20.** (i)(b), (ii)(c)
21. (b)	**22.** (d)	**23.** (c)	**24.** (b)	**25.** (d)					

Chapter 5   Adjectives

1. (b)	**2.** (b)	**3.** (d)	**4.** (c)	**5.** (b)	**6.** (c)	**7.** (a)	**8.** (b)	**9.** (c)	**10.** (a)
11. (b)	**12.** (d)	**13.** (b)	**14.** (a)	**15.** (b)	**16.** (a)	**17.** (c)	**18.** (b)	**19.** (b)	**20.** (c)
21. (b)	**22.** (a)	**23.** (d)	**24.** (a)	**25.** (c)	**26.** (a)				

Chapter 6   Articles

1. (a)	**2.** (c)	**3.** (b)	**4.** (c)	**5.** (d)	**6.** (a)	**7.** (b)	**8.** (c)	**9.** (d)	**10.** (a)
11. (a)	**12.** (a)	**13.** (c)	**14.** (c)	**15.** (b)	**16.** (c)	**17.** (a)	**18.** (b)	**19.** (a)	**20.** (b)
21. (b)	**22.** (b)	**23.** (b)	**24.** (b)	**25.** (c)	**26.** (a)	**27.** (b)			

Chapter 7   Prepositions

1. (b)	**2.** (d)	**3.** (a)	**4.** (d)	**5.** (c)	**6.** (d)	**7.** (a)	**8.** (c)	**9.** (c)	**10.** (b)
11. (a)	**12.** (c)	**13.** (a)	**14.** (b)	**15.** (c)	**16.** (a)	**17.** (b)	**18.** (c)	**19.** (c)	**20.** (c)
21. (d)	**22.** (c)	**23.** (b)	**24.** (d)	**25.** (c)					

Chapter 8   Conjunctions

1. (b)	2. (d)	3. (d)	4. (a)	5. (c)	6. (c)	7. (b)	8. (d)	9. (d)	10. (b)
11. (c)	12. (c)	13. (d)	14. (b)	15. (c)	16. (c)	17. (a)	18. (a)	19. (b)	

Chapter 9   Tenses

1. (b)	2. (c)	3. (b)	4. (c)	5. (c)	6. (a)	7. (b)	8. (c)	9. (b)	10. (c)
11. (d)	12. (c)	13. (a)	14. (b)	15. (d)	16. (b)	17. (d)	18. (b)	19. (c)	20. (c)
21. (d)									

Chapter 10   Active and Passive Voice

1. (b)	2. (a)	3. (a)	4. (c)	5. (b)	6. (c)	7. (b)	8. (b)	9. (b)	10. (b)
11. (a)	12. (b)	13. (c)	14. (c)	15. (a)	16. (c)	17. (b)	18. (d)	19. (b)	20. (i)(b) (ii) (a)
21. (i) (c), (ii)(b)									

Chapter 11   Direct and Indirect Speech

1. (c)	2. (b)	3. (c)	4. (b)	5. (c)	6. (b)	7. (c)	8. (b)	9. (a)	10. (a)
11. (a)	12. (b)	13. (c)	14. (a)	15. (a)	16. (b)	17. (b)	18. (c)	19. (b)	20. (c)
21. (b)	22. (d)								

Chapter 12   Error Detection

1. (a)	2. (a)	3. (a)	4. (b)	5. (b)	6. (d)	7. (a)	8. (d)	9. (c)	10. (c)
11. (c)	12. (b)	13. (b)	14. (c)	15. (d)	16. (d)	17. (c)	18. (c)	19. (b)	20. (c)
21. (b)	22. (c)	23. (a)	24. (b)	25. (d)	26. (a)	27. (b)			

Chapter 13   Sentence Arrangement

1. (d)	2. (b)	3. (b)	4. (d)	5. (a)	6. (b)	7. (a)	8. (d)	9. (b)	10. (b)
11. (b)	12. (c)	13. (c)	14. (c)	15. (a)	16. (d)	17. (b)	18. (b)	19. (d)	20. (a)

Chapter 14   Fillers

1. (d)	2. (a)	3. (b)	4. (b)	5. (c)	6. (d)	7. (a)	8. (a)	9. (c)	10. (c)
11. (a)	12. (b)	13. (b)	14. (d)	15. (a)	16. (b)	17. (a)	18. (d)	19. (a)	20. (c)
21. (c)	22. (a)	23. (b)	24. (d)	25. (d)					

Chapter 15   Synonyms and Antonyms

1. (d)	2. (a)	3. (c)	4. (b)	5. (c)	6. (c)	7. (a)	8. (b)	9. (a)	10. (a)
11. (b)	12. (a)	13. (b)	14. (a)	15. (a)	16. (a)	17. (b)	18. (c)		

Chapter 16   Idioms and Phrases

1. (a)	2. (c)	3. (b)	4. (d)	5. (b)	6. (d)	7. (b)	8. (a)	9. (c)	10. (b)
11. (c)	12. (b)	13. (c)	14. (a)	15. (c)	16. (b)	17. (a)	18. (c)	19. (b)	20. (c)
21. (b)	22. (c)								

Chapter 17   One Word Substitution

1. (c)	2. (a)	3. (c)	4. (b)	5. (d)	6. (c)	7. (b)	8. (a)	9. (a)	10. (b)
11. (c)	12. (a)	13. (d)	14. (b)	15. (a)	16. (c)	17. (b)	18. (a)	19. (c)	20. (b)
21. (c)	22. (a)	23. (c)	24. (a)	25. (c)	26. (d)	27. (c)			

Chapter 18   Reading Comprehension

1. (a)	2. (b)	3. (d)	4. (d)	5. (c)	6. (d)	7. (b)	8. (d)	9. (c)	10. (c)
11. (d)	12. (b)	13. (d)	14. (d)	15. (b)	16. (c)	17. (d)	18. (a)	19. (c)	20. (a)
21. (c)	22. (d)	23. (d)	24. (c)	25. (a)					

Chapter 19   Writing Skills

1. (c)	2. (d)	3. (d)	4. (b)	5. (d)	6. (a)	7. (a)	8. (a)	9. (b)	10. (c)
11. (c)	12. (d)	13. (d)	14. (b)	15. (a)	16. (b)	17. (a)	18. (b)	19. (d)	20. (b)
21. (a)	22. (b)	23. (d)	24. (a)	25. (b)					

Chapter 20   Communication Skills

1. (b)	2. (a)	3. (b)	4. (d)	5. (b)	6. (b)	7. (d)	8. (c)	9. (a)	10. (c)
11. (c)	12. (a)	13. (c)	14. (d)	15. (a)	16. (c)	17. (d)	18. (b)	19. (c)	20. (d)
21. (b)	22. (d)	23. (b)	24. (d)	25. (b)					

Practice Set 1

1. (b)	2. (d)	3. (d)	4. (a)	5. (c)	6. (d)	7. (c)	8. (a)	9. (d)	10. (c)
11. (b)	12. (d)	13. (a)	14. (c)	15. (a)	16. (d)	17. (b)	18. (a)	19. (a)	20. (b)
21. (b)	22. (c)	23. (d)	24. (b)	25. (a)	26. (d)	27. (a)	28. (c)	29. (a)	30. (d)
31. (b)	32. (d)	33. (b)	34. (a)	35. (d)	36. (c)	37. (d)	38. (a)	39. (a)	40. (b)
41. (d)	42. (a)	43. (b)	44. (b)	45. (b)	46. (c)	47. (b)	48. (a)	49. (a)	50. (c)

Practice Set 2

1. (c)	2. (a)	3. (a)	4. (b)	5. (b)	6. (d)	7. (c)	8. (b)	9. (a)	10. (d)
11. (c)	12. (b)	13. (a)	14. (c)	15. (c)	16. (d)	17. (b)	18. (d)	19. (b)	20. (d)
21. (b)	22. (c)	23. (a)	24. (c)	25. (d)	26. (b)	27. (c)	28. (b)	29. (d)	30. (c)
31. (b)	32. (a)	33. (a)	34. (c)	35. (b)	36. (d)	37. (a)	38. (b)	39. (b)	40. (c)
41. (a)	42. (c)	43. (a)	44. (c)	45. (b)	46. (c)	47. (c)	48. (d)	49. (c)	50. (c)